Lessons from
the Bad Kids

Lessons from
the Bad Kids

The Realities of Challenge and Inspiration

Vonda Viland and Deborah Turner

ROWMAN & LITTLEFIELD
Lanham • Boulder • New York • London

Published by Rowman & Littlefield
A wholly owned subsidiary of The Rowman & Littlefield Publishing Group, Inc.
4501 Forbes Boulevard, Suite 200, Lanham, Maryland 20706
www.rowman.com

Unit A, Whitacre Mews, 26-34 Stannary Street, London SE11 4AB

British Library Cataloguing in Publication Information Available

Library of Congress Cataloging-in-Publication Data

ISBN 978-1-4758-3314-0 (cloth : alk. paper)
ISBN 978-1-4758-3315-7 (pbk. : alk. paper)
ISBN 978-1-4758-3316-4 (electronic)

♾™ The paper used in this publication meets the minimum requirements of
American National Standard for Information Sciences—Permanence of Paper for
Printed Library Materials, ANSI/NISO Z39.48-1992.

Printed in the United States of America

Contents

Foreword

Truly successful educators are not just sculptors of clay, working with the raw materials of a student's strengths to help her achieve her potential. Truly successful educators must be equally attuned to what is sometimes a dearth of raw materials, to what in a student might be conspicuously absent. Absences, of course, are considerably more difficult to discern, and our failure to identify them is what allows so many at-risk students to slip through the cracks.

Not long after beginning our two years of filming at Black Rock High School, my collaborator Lou Pepe and I became fixated on an absence.

Kenneth wasn't absent in the conventional sense. Even though he was sporadically homeless, he somehow made it to school every day and managed to get to his classes on time. But his spirit was absent.

With his mane of long hair, hoody pulled tightly over his brow, and head planted firmly on his desk, Kenneth's face was literally absent. When he spoke, he did so with no inflection whatsoever and barely moved his lips. He didn't often smile or interact with others.

The one time I did happen to see a smile briefly cross his face, he was seated under a table in Black Rock's rec room, deep in the shadows and alone. He only smiled because he was embarrassed that I noticed him hiding there.

Curious about Kenneth, I started to ask the faculty members why they allowed him to remain invisible. After all, one of the tenets of Black Rock's philosophy that I had heard in student intake sessions over and over again is that students are not allowed to hide here. Hiding is what they could get away with at the mainstream high school and part of the reason for their failure there.

I was of course being naive about what the teachers had already been through with Kenneth. They had called him out on his lack of engagement many, many times. The teachers had conscientiously tried to notice him, tried to acknowledge even the slightest motivated or positive behavior from him. But Kenneth made it clear by his behavior that he was only here at Black Rock because it was a safe place to be. Safe, exactly because he could hide here. Very uncharacteristic for this faculty, the teachers, one after the other, admitted that they had given up on Kenneth. They just let him keep his head down and be invisible.

I then asked Principal Viland what she knew about Kenneth. Of the many traumatic stories that come through the doors of Black Rock, Kenneth's was one of the hardest to hear. His parents had been out of the picture for a long time, and Kenneth had been raised by his grandfather who literally kept Kenneth chained to a chair so the then ten-year-old boy wouldn't wander off and get into trouble. From ten to thirteen, Kenneth suffered this treatment. The few times he was unshackled, it was only to be dragged by his grandfather into the garage where he would soundly beat Kenneth, for what reasons the helpless boy never knew.

Principal Viland had herself tried everything in her usual tool kit. She'd spent hours in private talks with Kenneth, recommended outside counseling, tried to get him to seek housing and assistance from the local TAY (Transitional Age Youth) Center. Nothing seemed to work. When I asked Principal Viland if there was nothing more to be done to try to reach Kenneth, she looked crestfallen. This was one that was going to slip through her fingers.

The day after my conversation with Principal Viland, I was not at Black Rock. But at the teachers' daily meeting, Kenneth was the focus. The teachers were not accustomed to giving up. They were not accustomed to outsiders – me, in this instance – taking note of the fact that they'd given up. There were tears shed and considerable soul-searching. They spoke together about how they could give Kenneth one more chance and decided that it was at least worth a group intervention – something that they did with the rare students who were on the brink of being dismissed from Black Rock.

I also was not at Black Rock for the faculty intervention. But by the time Lou and I arrived back at the school several weeks later, something extraordinary had happened. Kenneth had _appeared_. He had cut his hair. He was not wearing a hoody. Passing me in the hall he said hello and smiled shyly. He seemed to have a purpose in his step, like he had things to do. He was *present*.

It sounds like the convenience of story-telling, but Kenneth's transformation was exactly this radical and something we became fairly accustomed to witnessing in the students at Black Rock during our two years of filming at the school. Students are capable of turning a dramatic corner when they are *seen*. Kenneth's absence had been so deep, such an impenetrable shell, that it was hard for the faculty to even let him know that he had been *being seen* all along. He was so used to being punished and humiliated that positive attention was not something he was capable of understanding.

When he heard from the entire faculty that they had been talking about *him*, that not only did they see him, but they continued to think about him after school and when they went home for the evening, that he meant that much to them, something switched on in his head.

It's always been in my nature to see the inherent good in people, regardless of how hard they try to hide it. And in Kenneth, I think I could see how the teachers' reaction to his absence had triggered the best in him. He was naturally a very polite and humble person. I think he hated the idea that he was wasting anyone's time or care. When he finally realized that so many people honestly cared about him, I think he very quickly started to feel that he mustn't disappoint them. The faculty's attention was an appeal to the sense of duty and good citizenship that Kenneth secretly harbored all along.

I spent a lot of time after this incident thinking about the notion of attention, both the kinds we pay to others and the kinds we expect to be paid to us. Much of the time the kind of attention a teacher pays to a student is predicated on the kind of attention the student is accustomed to receiving. In the case of the bad kids, this is of course negative attention. It's what they know, and they've learned the behaviors that can force the less patient among us to apply it.

Our temptation is to respond to bad behavior with punishment. And those students who are accustomed to receiving punishment practically demand it of us.

High schools like Black Rock specialize in moving beyond these bad attention cycles. They not only change the type of attention given to bad behavior, but they try their best to re-train the students in the types of attention they demand. As Principal Viland often said to kids, "You can play the victim all your life if you want, but if you keep acting like a victim, that's how people will treat you." With pity, not respect. With punishment, not recognition.

The absences to which a good educator most often needs to be attuned are the absence of self-esteem, the absence of a will to rise above circumstances that are generationally intractable, and the absence of hope. The problem is often that low self-esteem is something that so many young people suffer that it has become a target of cheap psychology solutions and the frequent application of that good old American advice: "Just pull yourself up your boot straps and get on with it. It's in your power to do so." Low self-esteem is very different, however, in this huge population of young people who lack the parental support and financial sustenance to get even the smallest foothold in our society.

When students start life already handicapped by trauma, hunger, abuse or neglect, we can't expect great results from just a pep talk or two. It takes a lot of time, the right kind of attention, and the ability to see what's deeply absent in a student to begin to turn that student's potential around. It takes a Black Rock High School. And for the millions of students in the United States who suffer poverty and trauma, it will take many more Black Rock High Schools and may more educators like the Black Rock staff.

Keith Fulton, filmmaker,
Lowkey Productions

Lowkey Pictures

Preface

The Bad Kids

There is a cadre of kids in our society, at every level, who need. Their needs are as diverse as our society, and it takes special people to address those needs. If these kids do not get their needs met, they become adults who search for ways to get those needs met. We know the stories of those adults. They become the homeless, the addicted, the mentally ill, the prisoners in our prison system, or even worse, the criminals outside of the prison system. But it doesn't have to happen that way.

Thankfully, there are places like Black Rock High School. Black Rock Continuation High School is located in a remote, rural, economically deprived, desert community. It is one of California's alternative schools for students at risk of dropping out.

The people in the community state it is the school where all the bad kids go, but in reality, it is the school where good kids who have been put in bad situations attend. Every student here has fallen so far behind in credits that they have no hope of earning a diploma at a traditional high school. Black Rock is their last chance.

As the principal at Black Rock High School, three years ago, I received a call from our assistant superintendent of curriculum, stating she was bringing a couple of men out to the school to see our program. When they arrived, they, of course, arrived at student lunch, the craziest time of day. It is the time when I get to touch base with all the students, see how their days and lives are going, and make sure they all have something to eat and drink, so I was a bit put off by the intrusion.

I was even more put off when I heard they were filmmakers who were interested in our school, so like all good leaders, I delegated their visit to one of our students, Daniel. I asked Daniel to show them around and introduce them to the teachers and the students, and show them around is exactly what Daniel did.

He began by explaining that Black Rock was the school for the bad kids, and he then proceeded to take them to individual students and introduced them by telling them the students' life stories. Jack was here because his mom was a meth head and let him run wild; Sally got kicked out of school because she was always getting into fights; Tom was homeless, but his friends were letting him couch surf; Keaton never did his work at the "other" school but was doing well here; and Daniel, well, Daniel had just been released from juvenile hall where he had done time for attempted murder.

I was sure I would never hear from the men again, but two weeks later, my phone rang, and it was Lou and Keith, the filmmakers of Lowkey Pictures. They said they couldn't get our school and our students out of their minds, and they wanted to come and visit for two weeks to see if the students would open up about their lives and their thoughts about the school.

I laughed at them and said, "Getting them to open up will be NO problem. If you ask them, they will tell you." I am not sure they believed me, and we agreed they would come out for a two week stint to "test the waters."

By the end of the first day, they were exhausted from following me around, but they were hooked, and they decided to self-fund a documentary, and the award-winning documentary, *The Bad Kids*, was born.

> *The Bad Kids* is an observational documentary that chronicles [my] mission to realize the potential of these students whom the system has deemed lost causes. The film follows [me as I] coach three at-risk teens – a new father who can't support his family, a young woman grappling with sexual abuse, and an angry young man from an unstable home – through the traumas and obstacles that rob them of their spirit and threaten their goal of a high school diploma. As [my] educational approach unfolds throughout *The Bad Kids*, viewers are offered a practical model for how public education can address and combat the crippling effects of poverty in the lives of American schoolchildren. (Lowkey Pictures)

It is my belief that all of us start life in a similar manner, but for some reason the bad kids' path down the road of life is redirected and ends up being quite different, and their stories need to be told. Wanting to tell the whole story, I approached Dr. Deborah Turner, an expert in elementary education, to help me tell their stories.

Their stories need to be told because we can all help, and we can all learn from them as we do so. There is hope if we work together and are able to address their needs at the exact moment when their need path intersects with their hope path. Their hope resides in each of us.

Rob Beckwith

Introduction

Lessons from the Bad Kids

Almost every teacher has experienced at least one of "those kids." The kids who won't sit still, who won't do their work, who don't attend, who won't conform to the classroom expectations, who are straight out defiant and disrespectful; in other words, most teachers have experienced the bad kids.

These are the kids who drive teachers crazy, who make them anxiously anticipate summer vacation. In all honesty, these are the kids who some teachers simply dread having in class.

Fortunately, for some reason, these are the kids to whom we have been drawn since the beginning of our careers in education. These are the kids whom we have grown to love dearly. They are the kids who have made us laugh, made us cry, and made us really think. They are the ones who have both challenged and inspired us on a daily basis. It has been a great privilege and honor to have been given the opportunity to work with these so-called bad kids.

Over the last thirty years, we have learned one major thing: If we take the time to listen to these bad kids and get to really know them, they will give us more lessons than we can ever hope to provide them. If we take the time to listen carefully, the lessons from the bad kids can teach us not only to improve our educational system but also how to become better people ourselves.

This book centers on the stories and the lessons learned from the bad kids. With a collection of over sixty years of experience working with them, we consider ourselves experienced learners; however, learning is only as valuable as the sharing of those key pieces of knowledge.

Whether in education or in our everyday relationships with others, the lessons the bad kids can teach us will make a difference. Their names have been changed, but their stories and the lessons they teach are still the same. Are you ready? This book picks up before the movie began – the stories and the lessons from the bad kids.

Lowkey Pictures

Chapter 1

The Power of Positive

While walking to an assembly one day, Carlos, an eighteen-year-old student who had recently come to our school, stopped me with tears in his eyes. I was immediately concerned, but he reached out to give me a hug and said, "I am so excited, Ms. V., I haven't gotten an award since I was in second grade. Thank you so much!"

At that moment I knew the mantra I had repeated over and over again, "The Power of Positive" was absolutely true.

Research has been quite clear that punishment does not teach or change behavior; it only punishes. The only true way to bring about change, to truly teach, is through positive interactions and positive praise.

And the most amazing thing about the power of positive is that it doesn't have to be a big token.

At Black Rock High School, we instituted a "Gold Slip" program where students are recognized with a written note from the staff for being productive, self-directed critical thinkers who develop and implement plans to become life-long learners.

Each day staff members write commendation notes to students for anything from making it to school on time to completing a very difficult assignment to helping another student or reaching their credit goal, depending on the student's individual level of performance. These "Gold Slips" are given to me to document, and I then get the privilege of giving the notes to the students, while giving them additional verbal praise for their positive behaviors.

Delivering these positive praises is truly the best part of my job. The impact of these tiny pieces of paper is simply amazing. The smiles that come across the students' faces as they are handed a "Gold Slip" and are told they are doing a great job is uplifting. I have seen over and over again the students who receive these slips increase their attendance and their performance in all classes, not just in the class from the teacher who initiated the praise. The impact is far-reaching.

Passing out these slips each day and seeing their impact on the students has taught me that positives don't have to be large or expensive or even tangible. The power is in the positive, not in its size.

A young sixth grade girl exemplifies this lesson further. She came to school dirty and bruised. She was very slight in build and not socially accepted by others. Susan was a little wisp of a thing that would disappear in a classroom; she actually counted on it. As a teacher, I would spend time with her, catching her up academically, but there was still a block.

In order to help Susan academically, I had to dig deeper. The time had come, as it eventually does with all students, to sit down and hear her story. Upon asking Susan about her home situation and listening to her, I realized that she was the caretaker for her small toddler brother. She fed and changed him, cared for him, and loved him, but school took her away from that role, and she worried the whole time she was away.

There was no father in the home. Susan had nothing but positive things to say about her mother, despite the fact that her mother had no job and no ability to take care of her children. Of course, the necessary reports had been filed and investigated with no findings regarding any missing basic elements: They had water. They had food on the day of the inspection. They had a roof over their heads.

In spite of the "no finding" results of the investigation, Susan knew better; she knew the true condition of their situation. In order to do her part to help, she would ask for any left-over food from the other students each day. When I saw this, I knew it was something I could address. If the authorities couldn't help this child, I knew of at least one way, I could help.

And so I purchased food and stashed it in her desk. I located a large backpack and gave her the backpack as a reward for her academic growth. I stashed more food in that backpack each night. Weekends were particularly difficult for Susan because there was no free or reduced lunch provided on the weekends, and so I stashed more food. Susan began to thrive.

Sixth grade girls love to pretend they are older, so I got permission slips from parents to have skin care lessons at lunch. Simple lip gloss and translucent powder lessons were also available, and I made sure Susan participated. After that day, Susan began to form friendships with the other girls who came. She started to take care of herself and concentrate on making herself better.

Then came the end of the year and the announcement that Susan and her mother and brother were moving out of state. My heart sank, but I was confident that our time together had made a difference.

Years later, over twenty years later, I received a letter from Susan. A letter that thanked me for the food. A letter that thanked me for helping her to be a good caretaker of her brother until he turned eighteen. A letter that thanked me for believing in her and valuing her. A letter that thanked me for having seen her as a person, not a problem, for spending time with her, for filling her with all that she *could* do, not what she couldn't do.

She thanked me because she had become a nurse and now a mother, and she knew that all her accomplishments had been built upon the foundation of positive energy she had received in my classroom.

It is an amazing thing to realize what the power of positive can do for a child. Sometimes teachers of younger students don't get to see what a small incentive, a little time, and a belief in them can do for their futures. I was very fortunate. I received so much more than a letter from Susan that day. That day, I learned that any small gesture of hope could intersect a need, and the power of positive could multiply.

Imagine what could happen if everyone realized that? There would be incredible power if we all expressed the positive in our daily interactions. I know we have one more nurse, caring for others, because of it, and in the long run, that is good for all of us.

Lowkey Pictures

Rob Beckwith

Chapter 2

Gifts

The bad kids teach us the importance of giving. Not only do they need and deserve our gifts, they give back to us on a daily basis. The gifts they give are everlasting.

At the beginning of my career, I had the opportunity to teach kindergarten. Teaching kindergarten is a gift in and of itself. It gives one the opportunity to experience creative innocence and enthusiasm. Kindergarteners are excited to be in school, they want to learn, they idolize their teacher, and parents are usually very involved. Unfortunately, that isn't always the case with the bad kids.

Darren, one special five-year-old in my class, walked three miles to school each day. He came dirty, hungry, tired, and unable to learn. He never smiled and usually walked with an angry scowl. He didn't associate with other children unless it was in an angry, hostile manner, and he was in trouble a great deal.

When I sat with him and talked, I learned he was very verbal, he had an extremely high vocabulary, and he could mentally do math well above his peer group. He was very bright, indeed, but he couldn't recognize letters or sounds, or write anything.

Darren ravenously ate lunch each day and would save extra food any chance he could as he had to feed his baby sister when he got home each day. His mother didn't get up until noon or later, so he had to get himself up and dressed and get to school on his own. Before he could leave, he first had to get his sister washed, clothed, and fed.

When he got home he needed to feed his sister again, but there wasn't always food in the house, so he would share with her anything he had been able to scrounge throughout the day. Darren took his parenting responsibility very seriously. He wanted the best for her, so he would sing the kindergarten songs to her, he scavenged the trash for extra coloring pages to take home to her, and he stole crayons and pencils to give lessons to her.

Darren could have been punished or received consequences for many of his behaviors, but by observing his behaviors and listening to him, one thing was perfectly clear to me. Darren valued his sister and was going to insure her success and survival. We could not justify handing out punishments for that, so instead we decided to help him on his parenting mission.

We assembled a backpack for Darren that included food, clothes, crayons, paper, pencils, extra workbooks, extra copies of our small decodable readers, and a wind up alarm clock, so he could start getting to school on time. He readily agreed when we asked him if he would like lessons about how to teach his sister to read and write.

We gave him these lessons during recesses and working lunches, and we promised if he got his classwork done, he could have additional lessons. Darren loved the attention, but more than that, he greatly appreciated the help he needed to be the parent.

He began to pay attention in class, do his work, and behave for positive reinforcement. We even taught him how to use positive reinforcement with his sister to get her to do what she was supposed to do. He worried about everything regarding his little sister, especially about her health and her need to go to the doctor when she was sick. We enlisted the help of social services and had him use the school phone to answer the questions they asked.

With our help, Darren became a very effective parent at age five.

Darren's story could have gone many ways. Being a parent is difficult enough for an adult, let alone for a five-year-old. Thankfully, Darren became a very successful student and ultimately convinced his mother to come to some of the school events in the spring where we were able to start working with her on parenting skills.

As a result of Darren's change, she began to change. As a result of the teacher taking the time to listen and observe and become the learner, the student became the teacher, for his sister, for his mother, AND for me as he surely taught me about the gift of what is truly important.

He gifted me the lesson of the importance of caring for and helping those we love.

In our society there is an expectation that certain basic experiences are had by all. For the bad kids, this simply isn't the case. Sometimes the most basic of experiences turn out to be the greatest gift we can give.

Each year, we try to take our students on field trips in order to provide experiences they haven't been able to have due to their life situations.

When I asked Jimmy whether he was excited to go to the beach, he looked disheartened and said he wasn't going. Surprised, I inquired why he wasn't going to go as I knew all the students had been chatting up the trip with great enthusiasm. He responded that he didn't have any money. I explained to him that didn't matter because I pay for all kids who want to go on field trips since we live in the middle of the desert, and I believe it is important for all students to have the opportunity to experience life outside our remote, rural, economically deprived, desert community. His face completely lit up, and he could barely contain his excitement.

The day of the field trip, Jimmy was so eager. He was first on the bus and grabbed the front seat. When I got on the bus, I asked if I could join him, and he readily agreed. He had his nose pressed to the window as we traveled out of town and "down the hill" toward civilization.

As we drove down the hill, I watched tears roll down his cheeks as he quietly sobbed. I grabbed his hand and asked if he was okay. He responded, "Oh, Ms. V, I didn't know all this was out here. I just didn't know." Until this moment, having never left our small, rural, poverty-stricken community, he truly had no understanding of the world beyond.

On another of our adventures, we took the students up to the mountains to experience the snow. Talk about a true feeling of bliss. Words cannot even begin to describe the experience of seeing a whole bus of teenagers experience snow for the first time. They laughed and screamed as they got off the bus.

The snow started flying immediately; then came the snow angels, the snow men, and the snow forts. For three quick hours, these students truly filled my heart with their innocent joy as they pranced in the snow, experiencing one of the true beauties of our great world for the first time.

This lack of life experiences sometimes would stymie our students, and they would need our gifts to get an even playing field.

The Walkers lived literally in the middle of the desert, thirty miles from the nearest town, and an hour-and-a-half from the school. They had no Internet or cell phones. They had two channels on their television that they received from a large antennae on their roof. They were a good family, led by their matriarch, Grandma Ruby.

She instilled in the kids a strong work ethic and belief in the power of a good education. In spite of the longer than an hour commute, her kids had perfect attendance. They were kind, helpful, caring, generous individuals who always went out of their way to help both staff and students.

One of the grandkids, Lesley, was an extremely talented artist. She would sketch and woodburn constantly; sometimes to the detriment of her studies. It was hard to redirect her to do what she was "supposed" to be doing because her creations were so beautiful. It was hard to justify tearing her away from such passion and beauty. Eventually, we were able to get her through the required curriculum, and she graduated. We worked with her to get her a scholarship to attend the Art Institute of California. She was so excited and so scared.

The week she was to go off to school, I received a call from her sister, stating she was worried Lesley wasn't going to go to school because she was too frightened to leave her grandma and the desert compound where she was raised.

I immediately came home from vacation, got a hold of Lesley, and convinced her that she could do this. I explained my faith in her and what a travesty it would be for her and her family if she didn't take the chance to tackle this opportunity.

I told her life was short and to always take each gift that was presented to her; if it didn't work, she could always readjust. I told her to always approach each opportunity with a "Why not?" I told her I would be there to take her to school and help her find her way.

When my husband and I showed up at Lesley's house to pick her up, she and her family came out of the house, carrying garbage bags full of her possessions. We helped load the bags into our van and headed into town on our way to the city. On our way, I slowly and quietly inquired whether she had bedding, towels, school supplies, and personal necessities. To each inquiry, she replied in the negative.

As we drove through town, my husband turned into the Walmart parking lot without being told. He knew we must open the door for this talented, young lady. He knew without our support her door would remain closed. She simply could not open the door on her own; it was just too big and too heavy a door.

Sometimes our gifts are premature. Our timing is not always in sync with a need. Sometimes, we give our gifts, plant the seeds, and allow them to germinate in their own time.

Even though our staff members reach out to all students and do all we can to make sure their basic needs and academic needs are met, each year, our staff members "adopt" a student to especially help. These students become like our own kids, and we seek to make a special difference in their lives each day.

One year, Jack was mine. From the first day he got off the bus, carrying his guitar, I immediately saw something special in him and knew he would be my "son." He was a scrawny young man who had a crooked grin and a sparkle in his eye.

He would often sit alone in the hallway, either playing his guitar or observing the other students. In class, he would put his head down, and the teachers would discover he was secretly reading when they went over to tell him he was required to have his head up and work. He would read classics and especially loved reading about philosophy.

Jack's dad had been in prison since he was little, and his mother vacillated between bouts of sobriety and episodes of meth use. She would go from times of not caring and being angry at Jack for getting in the way of her partying to times of trying to actually parent him. Jack resented both, but he especially despised the times she tried to parent him as he believed she hadn't earned the right to parent him, and like all teenagers, he wanted to come and go as he pleased.

There would be times when there would be food in the house, and times when he went hungry. There was the time she took the door off his room and threw water on him to get him up to go to school, and the time when she allowed her boyfriend to beat Jack up because she suspected him of using her drugs.

When he first came to our school, in spite of his home life, he attended school on a daily basis and did relatively well. I would hold counseling sessions with him where we would discuss his dreams of being a musician and getting out of our desert community. We would read *Adult Children of Alcoholics* together and discuss the similarities to his mom and his life. We would talk about the fact that there were a lot of homeless gifted musicians and that he really needed to get his education and "play the game" in order to make sure that didn't happen to him.

He was insightful and truly knew what he needed to do. He was an old soul. As we talked, he would often use the guitar to help him through our counseling sessions. He had an uncanny ability to sing his thoughts and emotions in rhyme to the music as he played the guitar, and I always enjoyed our talks immensely.

I felt really good about the progress we had been making, and I began to feel very hopeful for Jack's chances to graduate and move forward with his life. He did well with his studies and even earned honor roll recognition.

Slowly, however, the teachers began to notice a difference in Jack and would report to me that he would not do his work. They began to report that when he put his head down, he was no longer secretly reading; he was truly sleeping instead. He would refuse to put his head up or participate in the lessons. He would spend more of his day up in the office lying down than he would in class.

I would bring him in to talk, and he would tell me he had begun getting high again and that his mom was on one of her times of heavy use. He described parties in the house at all hours, no food in the home, and a complete mess throughout the house. We would talk and read for hours to no avail.

He began to attend less and less until one day he simply stopped coming. I became very concerned and called out to all the other students to help me find him. I called in probation and asked for their help, hoping to get him back in school.

Weeks passed, and one day, he appeared. I was so relieved to see him alive and gave him a huge hug when he got off the bus. When the bell rang, I called him into my office to talk. My fears were confirmed when he told me he had run away and was using meth. I pleaded with him to get help and told him how much faith I had in him. I offered him assistance and went out and got him the basic necessities.

I hoped that our school would be a safe haven for him and that he would see the diploma as a necessity to help him fulfill his dream of leaving the area. We spent hours together in counseling and tutoring sessions, but in spite of my efforts, Jack simply wasn't ready, and I eventually had to ask him to leave our school.

That day will forever be etched in my mind and in my soul as it truly was the one of the hardest, worst days of my thirty years in education.

I wept as he walked out the door, my heart breaking with worry and disappointment, but I knew I had to do it. I knew I could not continue to enable him and that I couldn't help him at that time because he simply was not ready.

People ask me why I would choose to include a story that demonstrates a time I appeared to fail or a "story" that didn't have a happy ending. The answer is quite simple; I have learned over the years that not all growth happens when and where we can see it. Sometimes we just need to plant the seeds and have faith that our gifts will eventually grow and then blossom.

Not all gifts have to be big or expensive in order to make a difference in a person's life. Sometimes, time can be the most precious gift of all.

Having had the privilege of working with incredible, hard-working, dedicated, caring teachers has afforded me the opportunity to see tremendous transformations in students.

Ms. Nicholls, for instance, had an incredible knack for making the person with whom she was working in the moment feel like the most important person in the world. No matter what was happening in her life and day, she would drop everything and take the time to work with a student in need.

Dylan was one particular student who demonstrated the power of the gift of time. He came to our school an angry young man who had not attended school for two years prior due to his life situation. He was like a wild horse – willful, defiant, and smart. When I met him and did his initial intake into our school, I was worried he wasn't going to stay long or that he was going to cause problems for both our staff and students.

I put him in Ms. Nicholls' homeroom with the hopes she would be able to work her magic.

His first day, Ms. Nicholls greeted him and welcomed him to her room. As was the procedure at our school, she explained that he was now her new son and that she would be watching over him.

And then she went to work, to work the magic of time.

Each morning, she would seek out Dylan to wish him a good morning and do a "check-in" with him to see how his night had been and gauge how he was doing with his anger and his general outlook. If he had been gone the day before, she would let him know how much she had missed him.

Each homeroom period, she would review his academic progress in all subject areas. She would praise him for his work and help answer anything with which he struggled or connect him with a person who could help him. She would help organize him for the next day.

She would then seek him out at the end of each day to say goodbye and tell him she looked forward to seeing him the next day to see what great things he had accomplished.

Each day, the "check-ins," work review, and goodbyes probably took no more than ten or so minutes total, but that time was the biggest gift of all as it showed him someone cared and he was worthy of someone's time.

After just the first week, Dylan started having good attendance, doing his work, and taking a positive leadership role in the school. After just a credit check of six weeks, he earned super honor roll status. His small successes had started breeding additional success, and he started not only making good decisions at school, but he stopped the negative behaviors he had been doing out of school as well. The gift of time was all he had needed.

Chance was another young man who was helped by the gift of time. He lived about twenty miles out from any civilization with his alcoholic mom. He was a quiet young man who when I first met him easily disappeared into a crowd.

He was one of those students who was easily overlooked by the system as he didn't cause problems and didn't have attendance or serious grade problems. He just came to school, did what he was told, and disappeared. He came to us after he became a little too far behind in credits to graduate on time.

When he came to Black Rock, he was soft-spoken and shy, and I worried he would be overshadowed by our kids who had severe family, work, and social issues. In looking over his records, I saw that he had tested exceptionally high on his standardized tests even though he had not performed particularly well in school.

Each morning when I greeted the bus, I made it a point to especially greet him and tell him how happy I was he had come to our school. I took the time each break to visit with him and ask him about his interests, and I took the time each lunch period to inquire about his day and his work progress and whether he wanted anything additional to eat or drink.

After a week or two, I took the time to give him a hug or two each day, and after a six week credit check, my husband and I took the time to give him a ride home after he had missed the bus and to take him out for burgers on the way home.

This relationship went on for the duration of Chance's stay at our school where he blossomed and excelled in all that he did. As he neared graduation, I took the time to help him with his FAFSA and his college application. I took the time to answer his questions and ensure him that he could do it, and I took the time to check in on him during his transition to our community college to ensure he had what he needed and let him know we were proud of him and would always be there for him.

As time passed, the cycle became reversed, and Chance began to give me the gift of time.

He would periodically take the time to "check-in" with me to see how I was doing and let me know of his success and accomplishments. He would call or stop by the school every so often just to say hi.

About six months ago, seven years after Chance graduated, my husband and I were having coffee in a coffee shop when a young, handsome man came up to our table and said hello. I looked up, and there stood Chance. I jumped up, and he gave me a big hug, picking me off the ground as he did. He had tears in his eyes as he told us he had just graduated with his PhD in biomechanical engineering, and he had been hired by the university to keep on with his research and to teach.

He thanked me over and over again for taking the time to notice and support him. He said that the gifts of time and support had made all the difference and helped motivate him to keep pushing forward.

Dylan's, Chance's, and countless other students' transformations did not cost money or require a great deal of intensive intervention services. The transformations only cost time and not much of it at that. Time is a small, powerful gift that will multiply and have a huge positive pay-off in the end. It is the one gift all of us can afford to give.

It is important to note that even though we may perceive ourselves as the "givers," in many instances in dealing with the bad kids, we are actually the beneficiaries of great gifts. The lessons they teach us are truly great gifts.

Often our past students will come in to visit and share their success or seek our help and support for work and postsecondary opportunities.

One day just before lunch, Elijah, a past student whom we had helped get into the California Art Institute under scholarship, walked in to say hi. As we hugged and talked, I began to look him over to make sure he looked well-fed and cared for. When I got to his feet, I noticed he had no shoes or socks.

As it was December, I was concerned and asked about his lack of shoes. He looked down and replied, "Well, Ms. V, I went looking for Jack as I heard he was having a hard time and living on the streets. He didn't have any shoes, so I gave him mine. I can always find a way to get another pair, and he needed them more than I do."

His actions made me think of Ashley whom I caught one day wrapping up her lunch and putting it in her bag. When I asked her about it, she explained that they didn't have much food at home, and she wanted to make sure her little sister had something to eat that night.

The generosity of our needy, at-risk students plays out each day with students sharing what little they have and helping each other survive.

Their generosity is demonstrated on a large scale each year when our students hold a canned food drive for our local Tender Loving Care organization. I always find the irony in this as here are the students who have very little themselves working hard to collect food items to give away.

The food drive at our school is always extremely successful as the bad kids truly understand that no matter how little one may have, they always have a lot to give.

The bad kids have taught us many lessons and given us many gifts. The gifts they give us are far greater than any gift we can give them. We can teach them how to construct a sentence, how to utilize the Pythagorean Theorem, or when and why World War I was fought, but they can teach us what really matters.

Whether it is the gift of helping someone help a loved one, the gift of joy from the faces of the students who see snow for the first time, the gift of time, the gift of giving one the opportunity to grow at his own pace, or the gift of the lesson that teaches us the importance of giving, their gifts far outweigh ours. Their gifts impact lives far longer than any academic lesson we can give ever them.

Lowkey Pictures

Lowkey Pictures

Chapter 3

Acceptance

There is something to be said about Baskin Robbins 31 Flavors of Ice Cream. So many flavors designed to appeal to everyone's variety of tastes. We all do not like every flavor, but we all certainly LOVE ice cream! This is the same in life. We may not like all individuals we encounter, but our lives are richer because of the variety!

At our school, we bring together all kinds and types. Our students are the people who march to the beat of their own drums; they are the square pegs that can't to be forced into round holes; they are the Skittles in a world full of M & M's. And that is exactly what makes them special – that is what makes them work so well together as a school. Each and every one of our students is special – each brings something unique to the table.

We truly are the perfect melting pot. I am often asked how I am able to bring together such different, at-risk, often volatile students, peacefully, and the answer is quite simple – we give unconditional acceptance.

When Randy started at our school, he was a skinny, quiet, withdrawn young man, who would hang out in my room, writing during the breaks and passing periods. One day, I asked him if I could read what he was writing, and he reluctantly agreed and gave it to me to take home to read.

That night I read about Randy, the young lady, dying to come out of her prison of a male body. I read about a great beauty dying to bloom.

The next day, I called Randy in to talk. We discussed all her thoughts and fears. I listened and let her release all she had kept pent up all her life. I asked about her openness to talking with a counselor, and upon her approval, arranged for an LGBT counselor to begin meeting with her and her family.

During the year, Randy slowly began to come out of her shell and present herself as her true self to the staff and students. The staff members enthusiastically embraced her and encouraged her to be true to herself. Our natural acceptance led to the students' acceptance. Each step she took on her path was accepted by all without a bat of an eye.

One day in a discussion with her, I explored the question of whether she had received any harassment or "bullying" at our school during her transition. She emphatically denied any mistreatment, saying that most of the kids had been "cool" with it. I asked her if she thought this would have been the same at the traditional school and whether she would have had the strength to transition there.

She paused for some time and then said, "No, I would have definitely been bullied there." When I asked why she thought it was different at our school, she said, "You know, Ms. V., we are all here for a reason. We are all different here. I guess we all feel like the 'freaks' of the district, and you accept us all unconditionally. We all have our own issues here, so we really can't justify giving anyone else crap for their issues."

The day Randy graduated was one of my most proud moments of my entire career. She walked the hall to Pomp and Circumstance blaring, wearing a long, red dress, long, white gloves, gorgeous black pumps, and a tiara. Every, and I mean EVERY, student clapped, cheered, and whistled. As they hugged and congratulated her, the acceptance and love that filled the hallway was immense and overwhelming. Her transition and success at our school was a display of the true power of unconditional acceptance.

This power was demonstrated over and over again during my tenure. Courtney came to us from the high school because she had been bullied, harassed, and even beaten because of her transition. She had basically quit attending school until she came to us. She was hesitant at first and would come every other day.

The days she attended we treated her with love and respect. We asked her opinions and asked her to fill leadership roles in the school. On the days she missed, we called her to see if she was okay and told her how much we missed her when she returned the next day. Within six months, she was attending each day, earning super honor roll recognition, and earning the highest recognition of the school, the Principal's Award.

Alicia was a young lady who had been harassed so much for her weight at the traditional school that she was planning on dropping out. She was convinced that all teenagers were cruel and heartless. She wanted nothing to do with anyone.

Once she started at our school and saw that no one was "bullied" or harassed for being different; once she saw that we celebrated uniqueness, she slowly started talking with others and making friends. She transformed into a super student and a super leader who was extremely popular. She had lunch each day with a table of students and talked and laughed incessantly like most teenage girls. She ended up doing so well that she graduated a year early.

In all three girls' lives, along with countless numbers of other students at our school, all it took was acceptance. It didn't take a lot of money or a fancy new curricular program – just unconditional acceptance. It is a powerful tool that will make a positive difference. We all want to be accepted for whom we are, and the best way to be accepted is to accept others for who they are – even when their choices and beliefs do not match ours.

When looking at the selection of over 31 flavors of ice cream at Baskin Robbins, some people are repelled by the appearance of certain flavors while others embrace that flavor due to its appearance. Preferences are subjective, and one person's dislike of a flavor doesn't mean it isn't a good product for Baskin Robbins. Baskin Robbins is successful because they have built their business model on EMBRACING variety.

When people walk into our school, they can often become intimidated by looking at our students. Our students are primarily male, and nowadays, it seems like they are growing them bigger and bigger. Because of their poverty, our students' dress is not always the best, and if one did not know better, our students could easily be mistaken as "gang bangers."

Reuben was a young man who could easily frighten an outsider. He was a very large, very muscular man who looked angry most of the time. When he first got to our school, not only did he look angry, he was angry, and rightly so. His home life was not ideal, and the school system had let him down in many ways.

It would have been easy for us to write him off and conclude he didn't care and wouldn't try or succeed, but instead we worked to find a way to hook him and bring him into our fold. We pulled many tricks out of our bag of tricks, and the one that stuck was, believe it or not, knitting.

One of our instructional assistants would work with our students during the breaks and afterschool to teach them how to knit. This originally started because she loved to knit and was convinced that knitting could have a calming effect on students and that it could help them keep their hands busy, so their hands would not be those idle hands that could become the devil's tools.

And boy was she right! She had started working with a few students and was seeing success when she took on Reuben. She first approached him when he had stormed out of class one day because he was angry at the English teacher for not allowing him to put his head down.

When he came up to the office, Shirley, our instructional assistant, sat and listened to him vent his frustration. She listened and empathized with him, and then she mentioned that one of the ways she stayed awake at meetings when she wanted to sleep was to knit. She grabbed her knitting materials and started knitting as they talked, and Reuben became mesmerized with the clicking of the needles and the fabric that materialized.

He asked what she was making, and when she said a blanket, he was very interested, stating that his little cousin could use a new blanket. When Shirley told him she would purchase the yarn for him to make his cousin a blanket and would teach him how to do it if he wanted to make one for her, he was hooked.

For the next few weeks, we would make an exception and let Reuben go up to the office to learn to knit; we figured it was more important for Reuben to form a positive relationship with an adult and that the required work would eventually get done. As Shirley taught Reuben how to knit, they would talk. They would talk about his past, his family, his thoughts and opinions, and his dreams.

Over time, Reuben and Shirley developed such a positive relationship that we started to see Reuben smile and laugh. His attendance became perfect, and he started to be a positive leader with the other students. By the end of the term, Shirley and Reuben had begun an afternoon knitting club that met for an hour after school each day.

Reuben had all his friends, who could have easily been out roaming the town, causing trouble, staying and learning how to knit. It was such a joy to peek in the room each day and see eight to ten big, young men, joking and laughing – and knitting. They called themselves the knitting gang and joked that no one had better mess with them as they knitted blankets, scarves, and toys for their family members.

The best part was the attendance, behavior, and academic work of all of the knitting gang improved immensely, and eventually all of them graduated.

Each time I fall in to the human habit of starting to judge someone based upon their looks or their past behaviors, I think of Reuben and his gang – his knitting gang.

Not all stories, however, have happy endings. And unfortunately, when one is in education, unhappy endings always concern students. If the stories aren't happy, they are most assuredly beyond sad because it is our children, society's children, who pay that price.

Johnathon was the class clown who had repeated this behavior for at least two years prior to being in sixth grade. It was his mission to make everyone laugh at him. He gave ridiculous answers, and his tween peer group laughed. He acted out in the classroom to prove himself silly. He embraced the attention.

He was filthy and smelly, had long shaggy hair, and was generally a teacher's nightmare as he couldn't maintain any semblance of learning due to the time he needed to spend acting the court jester. The other students made fun of his hair, his smell, his clothing, his apparent lack of intelligence. He was ostracized as he had proven himself socially unacceptable to other eleven- to twelve-year-olds, so the only way he could get attention was acting the class clown.

When I talked to him by himself and refused to allow him to act like a clown, he was bright and well-read. He enjoyed telling stories based on his favorite books.

Johnathon couldn't take baths because his family had to conserve water, and his house was heated by a wood stove that would both heat and smoke, making everything in the house, including Johnathon, reek of smoke. His mother never left the house, which also housed his much older sister and her children.

As the youngest member of the household, Johnathon only received attention when he acted silly. He also got attention like that at school, just not in a positive manner, but negative attention is still attention, especially to an eleven-year-old boy.

The staff and I decided to give Johnathon the attention he so badly craved in a positive manner, so I had him tell me his pants size, his shirt size, his shoe size. We collected money and bought the most stylish pants, some turtlenecks, long sleeve shirts, and sweaters. We bought a very expensive pair of name brand tennis shoes, new socks, T-shirts, toothbrushes, toothpaste, brush and comb, towel, washcloth and soap. We bundled it all in a new duffle bag with some classic books and a flashlight to read by.

He received it in the morning at school. He was so excited. He cleaned up and put on some very stylish clothes, much to the amazement of his peers. With his new look, his peer group openly accepted him throughout the day. There were very few instances of his CLOWN behavior that day! He integrated himself into the social network of the class, and for one glorious day, all was right. We sent the duffle home with him that Friday so that he could dress and groom himself each day.

Right or wrong, good or bad, people gain acceptance first on a visual level. It's the whole "first impressions" philosophy. This is very critical when we are learning about what it takes to be accepted by a peer group. Many tweens and teenagers do NOT find that acceptance for one reason or another, and they learn to seek it in any way they can get it, even if it is in a negative manner.

Unfortunately, Monday, Jonathan came back to school in his old stinky, dirty clothes. His peers were briefly confused, as was I. The positive attention he received the day before was gone. Students once again shied away from him, and so he chose to behave as a clown again to get attention.

We were puzzled and couldn't understand why Johnathon did not wear some of the clothing purchased for him, so in a quiet moment I removed him from class to ask about how he felt yesterday, how he enjoyed the company and respect of his peers. He agreed with me and thanked me again and again. He said it had been the best day of his life. He felt he was a part of the class. "Well," I said, "what happened?" Why didn't he wear the clothes? Why didn't he use the comb, the wash cloth, the soap? Didn't he like them?

I think I was shooting questions a million miles per minute; not even giving him a chance to speak. He lowered his head and just sat silently, his clown act having completely disappeared. When I was finished, he looked up with tear-filled eyes and said, "I can't wear my clothes you bought me. I don't have any of it. My mother sold everything at the swap meet for money." At that moment, Johnathon became a valuable lesson for me.

If we could all be more accepting and teach others to be more accepting, we could prevent a need to seek out attention in a negative manner. We could prevent individuals from being shunned for the style of shoes they have or the way they look.

I'd like to tell you I never bought someone clothes again – that there was never a need to help a student fit in due to his appearance. The truth is, there was, and I did – multiple times. As I tried to always remember the Hippocratic Oath, "First, do no harm," I learned to not send them home with the students. They changed into them when they got to school and changed out of them at the end of school.

Unfortunately, sometimes I had to work to level the field for a student, and with a more "acceptable" appearance, I could work with the other students in the class to be the model citizens of acceptance. I could teach that caring needs to go beyond what they see – a lesson we could all use to remember.

Baskin Robbins offers flavors they know may not be accepted by all because they know that variety will bring them more business. If we all embraced the variety of human beings, irrespective of appearance, our lives would be greatly enriched. The world would be a very bland place indeed if we were only offered vanilla.

Rob Beckwith

Rob Beckwith

Rob Beckwith

Chapter 4

Belonging

We All Need A Posse.

No one wants to feel alone. Life is hard even when one has a posse, but it is especially difficult when one feels isolated.

It is hard enough for adults to face life challenges alone; it is especially hard for teenagers who often feel alone and different from everyone else. As a result, many teenagers seek memberships in cliques, clubs, teams, and unfortunately, gangs.

Students who come from broken homes want even more badly to belong as they lack that basic familial membership. These students who have difficult life situations and who are not successful in school where memberships to clubs, teams and cliques are available will often do anything to feel like they belong.

DJ was a perfect example of this strong desire to belong. When he came to us, one could tell he was a "banger" by looking at him. He wore the LA logo, blue and bold, he wrote in tag, he walked with the standard strut, and he constantly doodled "LA" and "13" when he was supposed to be working. He "threw signs" every chance he could, used profanity every other word, and talked like a tough guy.

It would have been easy to classify him as a banger and just process him out in the name of keeping gang influence out of our school, but that went against everything the staff and I believed, so we rolled up our sleeves and got to work.

In our brainstorming session on how to best help DJ, we felt that counseling would not work with him immediately as he was unreceptive to change. As one of the staff members was talking about why kids joined gangs, we had an epiphany. We realized that DJ just needed family; he needed to belong; he needed to have his posse.

Our system at Black Rock is uniquely set up to create a family environment. Each student is assigned a "mom" or "dad" as a homeroom teacher who stays with them throughout their tenure at the school to act as their mentor and counselor. With DJ, we just picked it up a notch.

I greeted him personally each morning and met with him to see how he was doing and make sure he had all he needed. I bought him clothes that were not blue or LA, washed his clothes, and made sure he had food. I chatted with him about what was going on in his life and in the world in general, keeping it light and upbeat.

His homeroom teacher checked his binder each day and gave him positive feedback. She explained work he didn't understand and oversaw each assignment for all his classes. She talked with him on a personal level and reiterated how important he was. His core teachers gave him leadership roles and positive affirmation every chance they could, and we eventually put him in charge of our breakfast program.

It was not a quick or easy process. It challenged our patience. We would have good days, and then we would catch him tagging a book or writing in tag. We never talked about the "gang" behavior. Instead we focused on making him feel welcomed, supported, and appreciated.

We didn't let him get away with misbehavior, but rather than lecturing or punishing him, we assured him that behavior was beneath him and that we cared about him and his success and had faith he could and would accomplish great things.

It took quite some time, but eventually we turned the corner, and DJ stopped hanging out with his "gang" family and started being a full, participating member of our family. He even started referring to his homeroom teacher as mom, and he never wanted to let her down. He did his work, and like all seniors, he started to plan his future, finally deciding to go into the Army to join another family.

The day DJ graduated we held a big party just like a normal family does. We showered him with presents and reaffirmations that we would not drop out of his life just because he graduated.

A week after he graduated, DJ's homeroom teacher and I drove him down to the recruiting station for him to leave for boot camp. We wrote to him and sent him packages during his boot camp, just like a family would.

The day DJ came by the school in his uniform when he was back on leave was a proud day indeed. A member of our family had gone into the workforce, found his own family, and become a dedicated member of our armed services, proud and excited to work for our country. It was a true tribute to what one could accomplish with a posse by one's side.

We all want to belong to something or to have a posse of our own. In good circumstances, our first sense of belonging comes from our families, but that isn't always the case; sometimes we need to create that sense of belonging.

The first experience I had to create a family in an educational environment came from team teaching with another teacher. Team teaching with Cindy in a seventh and eighth grade combo class was one of the fondest memories of teaching I have. Not because it was easy; just ask ANY middle school teacher!

But, when one teaches in an area where there are very few two parent homes, where there are no employment opportunities, where drugs and their ensuing ramifications are rampant, and where kids are shot at and killed at a bus stop, teaching seventh and eighth grade is a special and rewarding challenge.

Cindy and I knew that we had our work cut out for us. These students had very little at home; in fact, few of them had loving, caring homes. Couple that with, and let's be real here, it's hard to be loving and caring with a child who has embraced puberty and all its negative manifestations.

They say "no" to every "yes" told them. They say "yes" to every "no" insisted upon. They won't do what is asked of them just because they want to see how the adult will respond. They test every part of one on a cellular level to NOT strangle them!, and that is what they do to THEIR OWN PARENTS! And if they don't have those, it's the rest of the world that gets those offerings of defiance and gifts of anger.

I was more of the disciplinarian on our team. Cindy was the one who would talk to the students and ask the important WHY questions, and she wouldn't stop until she knew why. She could wear them down by talking. The words I DON'T KNOW were banned from the class. We began to conduct our class like one large family of fifty-three. We taught our students to appreciate each other and support each other, and they grew to feel and act like brothers and sisters.

Teaching respect was more than a lesson from a book to us with our family; it was the lesson we lived and demonstrated every day. Indeed we taught the students a lot in our family, but I also learned a great deal.

I learned nothing gets past teenagers, and if you make a mistake, admit it. If you need to problem solve on your feet, do it in front of them and talk your way through it. They learn from our mistakes. When they make a mistake, ask why. They learn from their mistakes too. And I learned to never settle for I don't know. They do know.

Students referred to me as Dad, and Cindy was Mom. We modeled a functional home. There was discipline, dignity, respect, and an ever-growing groundswell of students who wanted to improve, personally, and academically. What we model as teachers can be at least as important and sometimes more important than what is modeled outside of the schoolroom. Together we were able to compensate for many of the shortfalls in our students' home lives. We were a family, and family is forever.

It has been seventeen years since that teaching environment, and our students, our children, went on to be very successful. There are so many success stories from our family: The student who had had to urinate in a balloon for her mother's drug test went on to receive her Bachelors' AND Masters' degree in mathematics. She is currently the head of the math department at a high school, teaching other students and forming her own families each year.

The student who came to us angry, defiant, and classified with special education needs, tested out of special education, graduated from college, and manages a restaurant while being a mother to her own five children.

I met one of my dearest, and yet angriest, former students in the ER not long ago. Both of us were there with our daughters. His daughter needed an x-ray for a twisted ankle; mine was curled up with extreme pain on the floor of the ER, practically unconscious.

He insisted to the charge nurse that my daughter and I go first to see the doctor; they would wait. He told her, "We were family, and that's what family does for each other." I was so grateful and so proud. My school son had grown into a kind, compassionate man. What more could a parent want?

What we do with academics is important to be sure. But we can also fill a need – a deeper need of being a part of a functioning family. It is perhaps even more important to raise our students to be great people, not just good students.

In our day and age, we have created an isolated world where everyone functions independently with their choice of technology. We have created the problem; it is counterintuitive for human beings to function effectively in isolation. We can clearly see the devastating effects of not developing positive connections.

We all need a posse, we all need to belong. If a family is not available to us, we need to create one. The sense of belonging we can create will foster positive outcomes for both individuals and for our society as a whole.

Rob Beckwith

Rob Beckwith

Chapter 5

Listening

When there is something wrong with one's head, the body sends out signals, giving one a headache and saying that something needs to be done to fix the problem. When there is something wrong with one's knee, a pain shoots up one's leg, yelling that something must be done to fix the problem. When something is wrong with one's stomach, one will get a stomachache so that something is done to ease the pain. When we have pain, we act quickly to try and relieve the pain. And when we don't listen, the body escalates the pain until something is eventually done.

The body's system for notifying us that something is wrong is much like an at-risk student. Often they act out to tell us that something is wrong and must be fixed, and they will escalate the behavior until we listen or they implode. Russel Barkley said it best when he said, "The kids who need the most love will ask for it in the most unloving of ways."

Brianna was a classic example. When she came to us, she was simply angry. Angry at everyone. Angry at life. Angry at herself. She would snap at anyone who looked her way or tried to talk with her, and heaven forbid anyone talk about her and she hear about it.

Due to her anger, Brianna was a fighter, and she had been sent to us after being expelled from the traditional high school for fighting.

When she first came, I spent hours upon hours, trying to get through the thick shell she had put around herself. She started to talk with a few people and to work a little with the teachers. I felt we had made some progress, but I knew she still wasn't letting me in completely and that her anger continued to burn beneath the surface. She still didn't trust me enough to get to the cause of her pain, and she continued to exhibit the symptoms in a lesser degree.

In spite of her progress and our developing relationship, I worried that something or someone would trigger her rage, and she would go off and get into a fight. I could feel the tension, but in spite of my efforts, I just couldn't break through.

Sure enough, she heard another girl was "talking crap" about her, and she got into a fight. I had to suspend her, but before I did, I talked and argued with her about her behavior at length. I let her scream at me, at the situation, and at life in general. I held her and let her cry until she was spent. She raged and cried until there was no fight left, and at that moment, I saw the shell begin to crack slightly.

When she returned from her suspension, I did not yet attempt to tackle the source of her anger; instead, she and I formed a partnership against her anger. We devised a plan on how to control it, instead of letting it control her. We developed a plan where she would hit a wall or a desk rather than a person when she was angry, and then we "graduated" to having her walk away and come to my office when she wanted to hit someone or the wall. Once in my office, I would let her yell, curse, and cry until the anger subsided.

This worked for quite some time, but I knew we were only treating the symptoms. We were not addressing or curing the cause of her anger. She wasn't ready. Sure enough, she lost control and eventually got into another fight. It was such a bad fight, she was arrested and put on probation, and I had no choice but to expel her from our school.

I cried during her expulsion hearing as it broke my heart to kick out one of my kids, especially this one. I told her I would welcome her back with open arms when the terms of her expulsion were met and that I expected her to quickly do what she had to do to return to us.

Six months later when she returned to us, I was determined to get to the heart of Brianna's anger. I was determined to cure the problem and not just address the symptoms, and I told her that her first day back. I told her we were going to dig deep and get to the bottom of the problem, and she was open to it as I had earned her trust by not abandoning her when she had lost control.

After that day, we met regularly to talk, listen, prepare for future possible situations that might trigger her anger, and to look back at times when she had lost her temper.

And then one day, we found it – we found the source of her anger. We were talking about parents, and when I asked her about her father, she began to cry. I sat in silence and let her cry, and then slowly I began to question her. She eventually explained that he was in jail, and when I asked why, she said, "Because of me."

Like so many victims, she was blaming herself for her father's abuse. She was hating herself because he had been arrested and sent to jail due to the condition in which he left her when she was a child and the severity of the abuse to which she had been subjected.

Once we had isolated the cause of the anger, we were able to tackle it head on, and we began to see a new young lady come to school. The new lady smiled, did her work, volunteered, made friends, laughed, and participated. She earned honor roll and eventually graduated early.

Brianna reminded us that we need to listen to the symptoms when they whisper, instead of putting them off until they have to scream at us to be heard. In education, if we would all take the time to listen and address problems when they are small, we could save a lot of students from having to scream to be heard, from having to escalate misbehavior.

In life, we could all save ourselves a lot of heartache and frustration if we would seek to solve the cause of our problems rather than chasing the cure to the symptoms.

Listen. It is one of the most important, no, CRITICAL, things one can do for another, especially with our youth. Not one of our bad kids wakes up hoping to spoil YOUR day. Not one of them goes to sleep at night plotting how NOT to do their homework. They do not look at themselves in the morning in the reflection of the bus window and say, "Today I plan to make everyone miserable."

There is something there – or not there – that has made these students cry out with their behaviors. They don't know what else to do. They are backed into a corner of wanting to be successful but not knowing how to do it. Listen to them talk, and they will tell you. They will tell you their reasons and their needs, regardless of their age.

George came to me as a first grader. His teacher had a litany of things George would not do. He would not sit still. He was not interested in the lecture by the teacher on reading. He didn't want to read. He didn't want to sit out one more recess for not doing his work. He didn't want to do anything in class, and he didn't want to be in a group – he hated his classmates.

He began starting fights on the playground where he wasn't supposed to be in the first place. He spent more time in the hallway than the classroom. Frustrated and desperate to find a solution before this first grader was expelled, I sat down next to him in the hallway one day and just listened. And learned a lot.

George hadn't gone to kindergarten, and he hated that everyone was smarter. He couldn't do his homework because the electricity in his home was intermittent at best, dependent upon the bill paying habits of his mother and grandmother. There was no heat except from a fire. His classmates said he smelled like a fireplace.

He didn't like that they made fun of him. He was in charge of getting his own food at his house, so frequently, when there was nothing, nothing was exactly what George got. He just wanted someone to accept him, but he knew people didn't and wouldn't, so he purposely gave them reasons to NOT like him.

After we talked, George began to wander down to my room during recess – he had to miss it anyway. As it was my prep time, I had both time and snacks. George was all over that! I started "sneaking" reading lessons to him. He was extremely intelligent and caught on quickly. He advanced two years in a fifteen-week time period. We did his homework together at school when I saw the burn marks from the candles and kerosene lamp he was using to read and do work at home.

I got him a clean set of clothes he could change into if he chose. He had to leave them with me each afternoon, but he could have them in the morning again. He started participating in class. By the end of the year, peer perceptions of the other six-year-olds had changed. George was the "smartest" kid in class. As success breeds success, he continued this through all his years in elementary school.

Unfortunately, while in high school, he ended up getting into trouble. Of all things, he broke into the school and stole some books. Parole assigned him a fine to pay, and he ran away.

It was around this time I became the principal of George's elementary school. Halfway through the year, George returned to the school. I was surprised and pleased to see him. We talked about what he would do next. He was going to enroll in the local college to get his diploma.

On his way out, he hugged me and gave me a piece of paper. He had written me a note. *I am sorry. Thank you for giving me reading. Please take this $4.57 for the window I broke. And thank you for always listening to me. I know I was a bad kid, but you listened and helped me.*

George wasn't a bad kid. He was a child who needed to be heard. A child who once heard was able to receive the support he needed to learn, and there is no doubt in my mind that listening made a positive difference in his life and can make a difference in any student's life. Sometimes we have to NOTICE when someone needs to be heard.

Take Kelly for instance:

As I greeted the students at the bus one morning, I noticed Kelly slowly shuffle off the bus with her head down, covered by her hoody. Being concerned, I asked her to join me in my office after the bell had rung. I gave her a hug and told her I had noticed that she seemed a bit down. That was all it took. We spent the next two hours talking about her being called into court to testify against her father who had both molested and prostituted her over the course of several years.

It broke my heart as she chronicled how it had been so hard to tell anyone, but that she had finally written a note to her friend, explaining that when her dad first started coming to her room, she told him she didn't want to be with him because it was weird because he was her dad, but she was afraid he was going to hurt her if she didn't.

The note proceeded to explain that her father had eventually sent his friend in the room one night instead of coming himself and that that pattern had continued with different men. Thankfully, her friend took the note to the authorities, but that did not end Kelly's nightmare.

The authorities needed her to help entrap the men in order to obtain the necessary evidence to convict them. Kelly was required to call each man and pretend she thought she was pregnant to get them to discuss the abuse. Kelly complied, and they were able to prosecute the men, but once again, Kelly had to relive the abuse by testifying at each man's hearing.

Needless to say, she was scared, angry, frustrated, and confused. She cried, yelled, and questioned. It was as if a volcano had erupted, and she was finally able to let everything come flowing out.

Kelly had all these pent up fears and thoughts and had never let them out simply because no one had ever asked.

A can of worms doesn't open up by itself. Human beings tend to internalize their issues and problems, sealing the can. We need to be the can openers, allowing students to share, vent, cry, agonize, and in the end, address their issues.

In doing my regular "check in" sessions with students, I called Leonard into my office to chat one afternoon. I told him I was so proud of his attendance and credit attainment, and he beamed with pride. He was so grateful I had noticed as he explained he had a plan and was determined to make it a reality.

His dad was in prison for murder, and his mom had run off and left him and his brother on the steps of a courthouse in LA. He was resolute that he was going to make something of himself and not fall into the same life as his parents. As we talked for over an hour about his feelings about his parents, his progression toward his diploma, and his plans for the future, I realized the true importance of having others care enough to "check in" and the power of having others with whom to share plans and create realities of our dreams.

Sometimes we also need to provide others the opportunity to safely seek information and guidance.

As we near the end of each grading period, I always ask the teachers to give me the names of students who could use a last push. I then call in each student to hear from them how they are doing and what they need.

During one of these checks, I called in Brad and asked him why he hadn't been earning the number of credits he usually earned. I saw the tears start to roll down his face as he quietly explained that he lived with his grandmother, who was the only caregiver he had ever known. He said that they had recently learned that she had Stage IV lung cancer and was given only a few months to live. He talked of how he was scared for her and for what would become of him when she passed, and then he looked up at me and said, "Ms. V, what do I do when I wake up and she is dead? What do I do with her body? Who do I call?"

We ended up talking for over an hour, and as I sat and listened to his fears and thoughts, I kept thinking, "What if no one had stopped to ask him what was happening or if no one had listened to him?"

People often ask me how I get students to open up to me and share their life stories, and the answer is quite simple, "If you listen, they will talk."

Rob Beckwith

Rob Beckwith

Chapter 6

System Failure

When I first think of system failure, I picture a complex circuit board in a massive computer panel of lights and buzzers in a science fiction movie when something is going to go very badly for someone very soon. There are many types of systems, and all of them can fail. When these systems fail, something WILL go very badly for someone, very quickly. This pertains to the educational system, and most certainly, to the schools and classrooms.

Tell me if any of this might be true in any adults' world

- You get fired because there was a coffee stain on a piece of paper at work.
- You get fired because your name was not on the right hand side of the page.
- You get fired because you turned in your work ten minutes late, and it was, therefore, NOT accepted.
- You were punished by your boss because you forgot your note from home.
- You were late, so your boss made you report to HR to document your tardiness, which made you an additional ten minutes late getting back to your department.
- You got fired because you misunderstood what your boss wanted, and he refused to repeat the directions.
- You got punished for being absent when you were ill.
- You got punished for having a bad day.

- Your pay was docked when you forgot to turn in your lesson plans/
  work, or your work was not complete at the precise minute it was due,
  so it was not accepted, and your pay was docked as a result.
- It is expected that you acquire all the knowledge you need to complete your project by someone lecturing at you for fifty minutes and
  then completing thirty practice problems. You can ask questions,
  but if you still don't understand, it is YOUR problem to solve. The
  lecturer has imparted their wisdom one time, and that is all they are
  responsible to do.

These are some of the expectations of the current educational system.
In this system with these rules, there will be failure; indeed, the system
is set up to encourage failure. As adults, we do not hold ourselves
to the same standard to which we hold students. We won't fail if we
don't get our lesson plans/work in by 8:00 a.m. We are not punished
for being absent when we are ill. The papers we turn in or turn back to
students may indeed have a stain or two on them, and, yet, the work is
still accepted.

It is right to set parameters for a classroom. Students, and indeed
most human beings, are most comfortable knowing what the parameters
are ahead of time. It is a system failure, however, if these parameters
are so restrictive and so limiting that any human mistake is fraught with
punishment and negative consequences.

Failing an assignment because it had a student name on the wrong
side of the top of the page is a failure of the system. Being even later to
class because the tardy policy says you have to go and report to another
place to get the absence on record prior to returning to class is a failure
of the system. When a teacher explains that they have lectured on a
topic, and it is the students' job to learn it, they are a presenter, not a
teacher.

In order to avoid the system failures, we need to ask what is our ulti-
mate goal. If we hope to "fix" our students, we must first fix these system failures because when there is a system failure. Something WILL
go very badly for all of us, very quickly.

Over the years, I have seen the system to be the reason students end
up at our school.

Take the traditional high schools' tardy policies for example. Time
after time, I have students who are tardy be assigned a detention because
they are tardy two or three times. If these students do not serve their

detention, they are suspended from school for defiance, which causes them to miss class more, which often leads to them failing their classes.

Yet in spite of the ramifications of the consequences, no one ever stops to question the students about why they are tardy or to really sit and talk with them to determine what is leading to their tardiness or their nonattendance at the detentions.

Now I understand that there are always cases of kids being tardy because they are teenagers and simply do not comply with rules or struggle to get up in the morning. I do understand that most tardies fall into this category. And I do understand the importance of teaching responsibility and skills for successful employment, but often our students, who get suspended for tardiness and failure to serve detention and who, therefore, fall behind, are not trying to avoid school, be defiant, or be irresponsible.

Take Arianna for example:

Arianna ended up at our school, labeled as a bad kid because she had been suspended so often due to her tardiness and failure to serve her detentions that she failed all her classes. According to the policy, Arianna had been afforded her due process and was justly suspended all those times. If anyone had ever taken the time to talk with her, they might have come to a different conclusion.

If one would have asked, they would have discovered Arianna's mom had passed away, and she and her older sister were raising the older sister's two kids along with Arianna's younger three siblings. One of the siblings was autistic, and one of the sister's children was in a wheel chair. Each morning, Arianna would get up at the wee hours to help get the other kids ready for school, feed them breakfast, get them organized for the day, and help them to get to their respective schools. She rarely even took time to eat or prepare herself for the day.

Because of these responsibilities, she was often late to school and would be assigned afterschool or Saturday detention, which, of course, she could not serve as she had to care for the kids. As a result, she was suspended so often that she fell behind in all her classes and eventually failed.

The only redeeming aspect of this story is it landed Arianna at our school where we greet students who come late with a smile and a "Glad you are here today." We take the time to inquire the reason for their tardiness without judgment. If we can't help to resolve the problem

causing the behavior, we accept it and commend the students for showing up in spite of their life situations.

One would be surprised how often this is the case with our students,
especially with our homeless students who don't have a bed in which
to sleep, an alarm clock to wake them, or a shower to cleanse for the
day. The system is to blame for these students' failure, not the students.

The system failing students happens to even the brightest of students.

Take Jacob for example:

Jacob was one of the brightest students with whom I have ever
worked, particularly in the areas of math and science. He could do
almost ANY math problem we could throw his way without writing it
down. He would look up to the skies and then spit out the answer as if
he could just see it.

And yet, Jacob ended up with us labeled as a "failure" as he failed
all his classes. Jacob just could not see the purpose for completing the
assigned work or homework, so he received 'F's on all of his assignments. He earned 'A's on all of his tests and tested at the highest range
on standardized tests, but because he didn't do the assignments, he
failed and was labeled as defiant. He never caused problems in class;
he just didn't do the daily work.

When Jacob came to our school and was told he could work through
the curriculum at his own pace, he was thrilled and extremely motivated. Once we tested him and realized his ability, we established a
curricular program that was specific for him, and for the first time in his
life, he felt in control and challenged.

The system was no longer holding him back, and he was free to run.
As a result, he blossomed and ended up graduating early. We assisted
in transitioning him to our community college where he flourished. It
was just a matter of getting the system out of his way.

We often assume that the system is clear and works for everyone;
however, we all know what they say about people who assume!

Over the course of the years, I have realized very few kids really want
to misbehave, very few desire to be a bad kid.

Even though the teachers have a hard time accepting it, one of the
reasons students misbehave is they simply do not have a clear idea of
the expectations or they do not know how to meet these expectations.
Teachers will argue this as they are adamant that they have clearly
explained the expectations numerous times, but we must remember that
kids' brains don't work as adult brains.

Brandon exemplified this point over and over again during his tenure at our school. Brandon was an exceptionally bright young man who seemed to have no common sense or foundation in the day-to-day world.

Brandon would come in late most days, and when reminded of the importance of promptness, he would sincerely apologize and reaffirm that he would try to be on time the next day.

Brandon would be sent to the office for counseling at least once daily because he would talk when he was supposed to be working quietly, leave the classroom more than the allowed number of times, leave without the pass or without permission, go into another classroom to talk to a student without permission, or work on different work than he was supposed to be doing at the time.

Brandon was never disrespectful or blatantly defiant, but the need to remind him daily of these basic expectations got tiring and irritating, and it was hard to convince the staff members that he was not intentionally misbehaving. Both the teachers and I grew frustrated with continually having to remind him of the rules and expectations.

After many months, many hours of counseling, and a great deal of frustration, I decided we obviously were not communicating clearly with Brandon. I simply did not believe Brandon was purposely defiant or disrespectful.

One night, while thinking of what to do with Brandon, the old life lesson that "You can't get what you want if you don't ask for it" kept going through my mind. All the teachers and I thought we had been asking for what we wanted, but obviously our message was not getting through, and I was determined to find a way to ask clearly for what I wanted.

So once again, I brought Brandon into my office and explained that I wanted to explain what I wanted from him one more time. This time, however, I did not sit and talk with him at length. I simply got out blank, colored index cards, numbered them, and wrote one expectation on each card. When were finished, we had eight cards written. I asked Brandon if he could do these eight things for us, and he readily agreed. I asked him to read through the flash cards three times a day – once in the morning at the start of the day, once midday, and once in the evening.

After he started doing this, we immediately began to see vast improvement. He was on time, he worked quietly when so directed, and he stayed in class. If he left, he always got a pass.

One day after seeing improvement for several weeks, I called Brandon into my office to talk with him about his improvement and his success.

In the course of our conversation I asked him why he thought there had been such a great improvement. To which, he replied, "I guess … because you asked."

And there it was. In life, you won't get what you want unless you specifically and clearly ask for what you want. For Brandon, that meant it had to be written out and reviewed on regular intervals. If we want our system to succeed, we truly need to make sure our requests are clear and delivered in a manner that can be understood by the receiver, and then, and only then, will we get what we want.

Every one of us can learn a valuable lesson from these students' paths. In education, business, and life, it is important for us to take time to reflect on the "why" we do things. We are often so busy, running from task to task, that we simply do things "the way they have always been done" or in the most expedient way, but we seldom take the time to analyze why we are doing things the way we are, or if our actions are getting the desired, best outcomes, or whether our expectations are clear.

If we did this analysis, we might find that we would get better results if we took time, asked questions, and did what we thought was best for each individual situation, rather than creating and using systems that get things done efficiently, but don't necessarily lead to the best results.

Rob Beckwith

Rob Beckwith

Chapter 7

Failure is Not an Option

Unfortunately, sometimes kids don't know anything but failure. Sometimes they need to be shown how to use the tools they have to be more than a failure. Sometimes they need to be shown that success is waiting; they just need to refuse to fail. They need to be shown that success really IS an option.

Frank was almost fourteen and still in an elementary school when he transferred into our school from another state. His sister had dropped out of school in ninth grade, and he had already failed at least one grade that we knew of, but more likely he had failed two. He lived with his mother and sister in an old cabin that a landlord ran.

Frank came to my attention when his teacher declared she could no longer have him sit in her class and do nothing. She was frustrated as he had been asked to do a Science Fair project and had done absolutely nothing, so she sent him to me for counseling.

Into my office Frank strutted. He told me I couldn't make him do anything. He didn't care if he failed. He hated his teacher and school in general. I told him all of those things were true and understandable. He was right. I asked him why he wanted to fail. He looked at me with dismay and said he didn't WANT to fail; it was just what was expected. It was what he did.

I asked him if he ever thought about what he could do if failure weren't an option. I also asked him if he would stay after school if I would work with him to help him succeed. He reluctantly agreed, but he didn't think he could be successful; it wasn't what he did.

We started with the Science Fair project. Usually in most schools, this is something that is assigned and worked on at home with supportive parents. With Frank, it would be done after school with me. He went through a litany of possibilities and finally found something that truly interested him. He conducted the experiment and several trials. He learned to use the computer to record his work and to type and save it.

He came to me one day and indicated that he had finished his science for the day and asked if he could use the computer to type his vocabulary words and definitions for his English class. "Absolutely." His teacher began to notice Frank would turn in work; not consistently, but at least two out of three assignments. One day he came to me after school as I was vacuuming the office area and asked if he could do the vacuuming. His work was completed, and he liked to vacuum. "Absolutely." Can he do it every day? Once his work was done? "Absolutely."

The next morning, I entered school two hours prior to opening as I usually did. Frank was there. He had walked from home. He said there was a lot more of the school that needed to be vacuumed. One hour into his vacuuming, Frank came to me in tears. He indicated that the landlord had thrown his family out the previous night, and they had spent the night on the porch. I asked him if his mom was looking for another place to live. Frank said she had no money, and no one would rent to them. He sat in my office and screamed and cried that nothing ever worked out, that everything always turned out badly.

After getting him calmed down, I asked him if he really liked the place he was getting kicked out of. "Nope" – he hated it. "Well, this might be the opportunity to jump into something better," I said. I made a few calls and by the afternoon, Frank and his mom and sister had a place to stay for a week until they could make arrangements to sign the paperwork to rent a place of their own.

Frank continued to come early for the rest of the year. He continued to stay after school. He walked both ways. He continued to do his work, and he continued to vacuum. He did not, however, continue to fail as that was no longer an option for him.

At the end of his tenure with us, through the assistance of a group of very dedicated teachers, he made it into a residential, elite boys' academy. His parting words on his last day to me were, "I will be successful … because it's what I do now." And he smiled as he walked out toward his next journey.

Sometimes parents want more for their children. They do not want their children to fail as they perceive they themselves have.

The mother sat crying in my office. Her twin girls were in second grade, and she was being abused by her husband. They had been drug users for a long time, but she knew it was time to quit. He didn't want her to quit and would physically demonstrate that anger with her. She suffered from bipolar disease and had always self-medicated, but the time for illegal drug use had run its course in her life, and she wanted a better one for her daughters.

Yet, she was trapped; she had nowhere to go. She couldn't be around him, and she certainly didn't want to expose her daughters to any more of the abusive behavior. I gave her tissue after tissue. And some phone numbers. She looked at me and told me if she didn't leave, her girls would suffer her same fate, and she knew that failure was not an option.

As fate would have it, her mother needed her help with her ailing father, so her parents moved to be closer to her. She and her daughters were able to move in with them. It was the perfect situation: Grandma helped with the twins; mom helped with her father. In spite of the move, unfortunately, the abusive husband took things one step too far and ended up in jail. With our guidance, mom began to see a therapist and got her daughters into therapy as well. The school staff rallied behind the girls and got them extra tutoring to help with their learning deficiencies. The past was no longer going to take hold of these girls' futures.

Years later, invited to Black Rock's formal graduation to give the speech, I was grabbed from behind. There was mom and grandma hugging me and saying with pride that the girls were graduating that night. The twins had plans, one to go to the local community college, the other off to serve the country in the military.

The mom and grandma beamed with pride at all they had come through, all that the girls had faced and conquered. I gave the speech and met them afterward. There were two of the most beautiful women, their mom, their grandma and all of them crying. I gave out tissue after tissue, but this time, I saved one for myself.

There will be students who will have to face more in the first years of their lives than we will have to face if we had four lifetimes. Sometimes they need just one person in their life to say, "You can create the life you want – failure is not an option." Sometimes, they need encouragement. Sometimes they need a little extra help. Sometimes they need a personalized feel to their education to help them over the large mountains that are difficult to scale. And sometimes, they need you and a tissue to say, "YES. You can do this. The past does not have to predict your future."

As human beings, we don't always learn things the first time, and we don't always succeed the first time. Sometimes we must try, try again. This is not just the case with our students; we adults need to recognize that failure is not an option for us either. We simply cannot afford to fail as our failures would have too far reaching of an impact.

In our line of work, we don't get the comfort of knowing if we do x, y will happen. It is not like a factory where we put in all the pieces and come out with a perfect final product. We deal with hundreds of various wills and spirits, hundreds of different influences, and hundreds of different life situations each day, each minute. And that is no easy task. It can be frustrating and exhausting, and yet, my teachers face these variables each day, and in doing so, have taught me many lessons.

Danny would show up to Ms. Friedman's class late each day and refuse to do any work. As soon as he got there, he would grab the bathroom pass and head out the door again. Using these tactics, he was able to pass almost the entire period without getting any work done.

After trying many things, Ms. Friedman created a policy for all students, stating that if they were late to class, they couldn't leave for any other reason throughout the period. The first day, Danny showed up late and tried to leave with the bathroom pass, Ms. Friedman reminded him of the policy.

He tried to argue and asked for me to come down to mediate. I listened to both he and Ms. Friedman and then supported Ms. Friedman's policy as it had been discussed with all students, including Danny, previously. Everyone knew the expectation, and therefore, the expectation would be upheld.

For the next week, Danny showed up on time each day for the first time all year, and Ms. Friedman celebrated his growth both with Danny and with our staff. She had found the solution to getting Danny to class on time and had begun to formulate a relationship with him.

A week later, Danny showed up late again and didn't get anything done during the period. When she wouldn't let him leave for the bathroom, he spent the period, getting out his work, looking for a pencil, sharpening his pencil, and wasting time as best he could. At that moment, Ms. Friedman could have thrown up her hands in frustration and given up on Danny, but she didn't; instead, the next day, she had out pencils and pens, paper, a book, and all Danny needed in his area, so even though he came in late, he could get some work done.

And for a few days, Danny would get to work when he got there, and Ms. Friedman celebrated his growth with Danny and our staff. She had found the solution to getting Danny to do his work and had begun to formulate a relationship with him.

A week later, Danny was back to being late and trying to get out of class with the bathroom pass. Once again, Ms. Friedman could have thrown up her hands in frustration and given up on Danny, but she didn't; instead, she met with him and asked why he was coming late and avoiding work. At this meeting, Danny started out by saying he hated science, and after some time and much discussion, finally he admitted he didn't understand the work – the reading was just too difficult.

Ms. Friedman heard what he was saying and worked to modify the curriculum and work for him, so he could get the content of the curriculum without the difficult reading, and she thought she had it. She celebrated her success with both Danny and the staff as he started showing up on time and doing the work.

Once again, it would be nice to say that Ms. Friedman was able to transform Danny, but with Danny, once she would address one problem, another would appear. It was like watching a balloon be squeezed at one end and then another. She would squeeze, and Danny would pop out at the other end.

To Ms. Friedman' great credit, she didn't give up; she would just squeeze again in another space. Watching this dance between Ms. Friedman and Danny, and the other teachers with numerous other students, reminded me that in life we all need to try, try again. If we do, ultimately, we will make a positive difference in both others' and our own lives.

Rob Beckwith

Lowkey Pictures

Chapter 8

The Power of Our Words

As an old English teacher, I have long been convinced of the power of our words. If one stops to listen to why many of the bad kids' reasons for ending up at the continuation school, he/she will know that it is definitely NOT true that "sticks and stones may break my bones, but words will never hurt me" because words can and do hurt.

Anthony was a perfect example of this.

Anthony came to us midway through his junior year. He had earned fifty of the required 220 credits, classifying him still as a freshman. While reviewing his academic record, I noticed Anthony had always scored advanced and above grade level on every standardized test, but since fourth grade he had earned abysmal grades. There were comment after comment, stating Anthony was defiant and absolutely refused to follow directions or complete any assignment. I was interested to see how he would perform at our school.

His first grading period, I just observed. He appeared disengaged and apathetic to all directed and contract assignments. He would read all day long but would do very little work. Both his homeroom teacher and core teachers explained that he could work at his own pace and could get the work done and move on with his life if he wanted.

We explained the system over and over again; if he hated school, he should just do the work and be done with it. We offered him assistance. We offered him incentives. We included his aunt in hopes of persuading him. We tried peer partners, pressure, and patience. Nothing seemed to work, and we neared the end of his senior year with little progress.

Great attendance, a great number of books read, little credit, and great frustration on the part of the staff members. None of our tricks had worked, and I could have written one of those comments in his records and moved him out.

In spite of having already had numerous conferences with Anthony to no avail, I decided to have one last conference with him in hopes of obtaining a commitment on his part to do the work if I invited him back for a fifth year. There was little doubt in my mind he could do the work; it was just a matter of whether he would finally put forth the effort to do it.

So, I took a deep breath and called him into my office one more time to talk. After initial chit chat, I asked Anthony what he felt the cause of his not doing any work was. He responded, "Uhh, I would say the cause would be complete indifference. I just don't care. I like learning things. I just don't care to put forth the effort to do the requirements."

I pressed, "But why?"

There was a long pause. It took all I had to keep quiet and let the pause fill the space. Eventually he said, "I remember sometime in fourth grade my teacher told me I would never amount to anything, so I thought everything I did was for no reason. And I realized it didn't matter what I did. I would never amount to anything, so why bother?"

I sat there dumbfounded. As my eyes welled up, I said, "I am so sorry, honey. I am so sorry that your teacher didn't see the true you – that she did not see all the great potential inside of you. I am so sorry that this teacher took away your joy of doing the school thing. I am so sorry that teacher did not see you the way I see you for I see a young man who is smart and insightful, a man who is certain to accomplish all he sets out to do, a man who can do great things if only he puts forth the effort."

After much give and take, I finally said to him, "You have given your fourth grade teacher's words much power over your life for the past eight years; how about giving my words just as much power for the next year? How about you live according to my perception and my words for just one year and see what happens? What do you have to lose?"

As he left, he hugged me and said, "I'll think about it, Ms. V. I'll think about it."

The next day when I was visiting classes, I noticed Anthony in his English class actually doing his work rather than reading. I touched his shoulder and kept moving, not wanting to curse the situation.

At the next weekly staff meeting when we got to Anthony's name, Anthony's homeroom teacher had nothing but praises. She said he had completed his plan folder and had earned credit in all subject areas that week. She couldn't believe the transformation.

This pattern continued until the end of the year when I invited him in to give him his fifth year contract. As he signed the contract, he looked up and said, "I decided to give your words power for a year, Ms. V. Let's see where this ride takes us."

I am glad to say the ride took Anthony to an early graduation the following year and a start at our community college.

Anthony's ride should remind teachers and non-teachers alike that we must always proceed with great care, great caution, especially when we are frustrated or having a bad day. One little slip can change the course of another's life for "sticks and stones may break one's bones," and words CAN also hurt. The injuries caused can last a lifetime.

Sophia was a student who attended school before bullying became a front page event and a deep concern for many of us. Bullying and how to address it were not discussed in teacher preparation courses, professional development, or in blogs, but rather victims depended upon the heart of concerned adults.

Sophia was a student of mine who was loved dearly by her family. Both of her parents were involved in her life and valued education, so Sophia studied hard in school and excelled academically. She was a people pleaser who would always do what she was told.

One would wonder how she could possibly be included in a *Lessons from the Bad Kids* as she was definitely not a bad kid. Unfortunately, she is a student who teaches her lesson from another perspective. She was the victim of the bad kids, and her story definitely deserves to be told.

As Sophia was overweight for her age, she didn't have many friends. Children wouldn't socialize with her and would taunt and torment her when there were no adults around to protect her. We did our best to look out for Sophia and make sure no one would tease her in our presence, but we could only protect her when she was with us as she would never complain or let us know what was happening even though the power of words had begun to inflict their injury on her.

We expressed our concern to her parents who wanted to help her, but they really couldn't do anything from home, and they certainly couldn't force the students to be kind. We teachers rallied around Sophia to help her try to form friendships, pairing her up in teams and partners who we thought would be kind and welcoming to her, but, unfortunately, this didn't always work.

Students would audibly groan when paired with Sophia, so she learned to work alone and excelled on her own. Recess and PE teams would choose her last, and Sophia would do her best to disappear, but she didn't have magic powers, and that wasn't always possible.

Picture day was one of those times she couldn't disappear. Elementary school photographers would often give cute nick names to the students when they took their pictures – cutie-pie, princess, Superman. The students were always very excited about picture day, and everyone would compare notes about their nick names in the classroom when they returned.

When a student asked Sophia what the photographer had called her, she proudly said, "Butterball," thinking it was a term of endearment. The group around her laughed and laughed and pointed at her, making fun of her. She hadn't realized it was a derogatory term, and she sat at the back of the class as the kids laughed and tried to disappear. The power of words had injured her once again.

Thankfully Sophia was an intelligent young lady who had a family who loved her and teachers who cared. She threw herself into her books because they were a safe way to escape. She dreamed of being a teacher and helping little girls like herself.

Despite what the staff and I could do, she didn't really develop any friends. In an effort to get her involved, we got Sophia to take up band, and she was able to develop a group of acquaintances who were also perceived as misfits. She and this support system left us for the junior high, and we felt comforted that we had been able to help her find a niche and a group of students who would support her.

But, unfortunately, our protection could not follow her to junior high or high school. Some of our kids would come back and fill us in as to what was going on in the high school with our previous students, and when they told us of Sophia, the stories were not always good.

Sophia had become a target of the upper classmen. They called to her in the hallways, said she wasn't born, she was hatched, or perhaps dredged up from the scum at the bottom of the ocean. They told her that her mother didn't love her, that she was just waiting to get rid of her. When she was in uniform at PE, they would steal her street clothes. They tagged her locker with words like FATSO, UGLY, WORTHLESS.

The students said her grades were good; she was at the top of the class, but she really only socialized with the band geeks. I gave a moment of thanks that we had been able to convince her to join the band and that they had continued to support her. I was also thankful that she had set a goal that she was determined to reach – she wanted to be a teacher to help students like her be protected from the negative power of words.

One day, she showed up in my office to visit. I asked her about the things the students had reported to me, and she admitted to all of the name calling and targeting. I asked if she had told her mother and father. Sadly, she had come to believe the words that were thrown at her; she had begun to believe she wasn't worthy, and she also felt she shouldn't add to her parents' burdens.

I tried to convince her of how beautiful she was. She had all the characteristics that would serve her well in life. She was friendly, caring, dedicated, intelligent, and kind. "The other students simply must be jealous," I said. Sophie thanked me and promised to keep up correspondence while at college.

Sadly, Sophia continued to be the victim of the hurtful words into her adulthood. Not knowing how to make friends and talk with people her own age, Sophia didn't do all the social things that other college students got to do. She didn't go to the parties, she didn't hang out with friends on campus, she didn't go on dates. Females tended to shun her, and the only male interest was negative. She dressed in layers of clothing to "hide all the faults of her body" of which the negative words had convinced her.

She got a job to pay for her classes and studied hard to pursue her goal of becoming a teacher. She was determined to be a teacher. She volunteered in classrooms near the college with any moment she could find.

In these classrooms, she found unconditional love from the little children. She was adored by students and staff alike. She was accepted for herself; for the first time her weight didn't matter, and there were no hurtful words. She began to shine.

She wrote to me to tell me all about the lessons she was getting to do, about the students she was helping, and about the joy she was experiencing in doing it. She had even found a job in teaching after she graduated. She had finally found a cure for the hurtful words.

In this instance, our lesson was from the victim. Sophia certainly felt the pain and internalized it. The power of those kids' words was hurtful and long-lasting. Thankfully, in this case, Sophia had the support from her teachers and family, and she had the determination to use the hurt to project her toward a future where she could help others in her situation.

She had the gumption to move forward, and she is a great teacher. So many of our students, whether from the influence of words from adults or words from other students, take a different path from Sophia and give up or find negative outlets for their hurt. As a society, we cannot believe in the sticks and stones adage. Words once spoken can indeed have a profound effect on others – for good, or not – and we all need to be sensitive to that whether in the classroom or in life.

By the way, as an aside, Sophia still loves teaching after quite some time in the profession. The beautiful soul that was always hidden inside has emerged, and she continues to help all students, especially the outcasts.

Rob Beckwith

Rob Beckwith

Chapter 9

Rich Resiliency

Resiliency: the ability to recover rapidly from illness, change, or misfortune. This characteristic is most important in the life of the bad kids for often they have been given more than their share of illness, change, and misfortune. Sometimes, kids are so resilient that they are able to make good decisions, in spite of all that life throws their way, and avoid becoming one of the bad kids. These kids' stories should also be told as they too can teach us a valuable lesson.

Ralph was one of those kids who certainly had more than his share of misfortune and change. He was a highly gifted and creative student of mine who had been dealt a bad hand and who could have easily become one of the bad kids.

His single parent mom was a drug user on and off, who went in and out of rehab, so he was primarily raised by his grandma and her boyfriend. He saw his mother off and on when she returned from rehab, but she was still deeply involved in the drug culture. Ralph's grandma and her boyfriend raised Ralph as best they could, having him attend school and learn proper social skills, but they had to relinquish control each time mom came back.

By the time Ralph was ten, he operated in two worlds – the traditional world of his grandmother and the world of the drug culture of his mother, and even at his young age, he knew it. Thankfully, he was resilient and was able to quickly learn the appropriate behaviors to survive in both worlds. He could clearly delineate the needed behaviors to operate successfully in both.

In spite of his mother's influence, he had made the connection between education and success and always worked hard to remain on the honor roll. He would find a way to get the work done, using his recess time if necessary, since he was often unable to get the work done at home when his mother was in the picture.

Not only did Ralph have to overcome his mother's drug addiction and having to bounce back and forth between the two worlds, his grandmother's house burned down when he was in fourth grade. We at the school, Ralph's friends, and the community rallied behind the family, donating clothes and a temporary place to live until insurance came through. Once again, in spite of the hardship put on Ralph and his family, he continued to excel in school.

Around this time, Ralph had an epiphany, and informed everyone that he planned to be a lawyer. He seemed to intrinsically know that he would have to create a future for himself, for if he didn't, he could become one of the bad kids. He was determined not to let that happen.

Ralph seemed to realize that in order for him to succeed, he would have to surround himself with positive people outside of the home, since he couldn't count on that support from home. He developed good friendships at school and was greatly liked by many. He led this "scholarly" group in supporting one another to do well in school. The staff and I encouraged this group, especially Ralph, hoping that life would give him the blessings he so deserved.

But sometimes, life deals some people a worse hand than others, and his grandma's new husband died, leaving grandma in a state of constant depression coupled with the effects of age. Once again, Ralph would have to reach deep inside himself to keep on the right path for now he had absolutely no reaffirmation in the home. He would have to not only parent himself, he would have to care for both his mother and his grandmother. It wouldn't have surprised any of us if he had just given up in school, but he didn't.

Ralph continued on. He reached out for assistance and sought positive relationships in peers and adults. When he made it into the Advanced Placement classes in high school, he sought the support where he knew he could always get it; he came back to his elementary school to use the library and computer lab for studying, as it was closer to his home than the high school, and he knew we would be there to support him.

Ralph excelled, and as he neared graduation, we again assisted him as he didn't have the support that the other seniors had for matriculating to college. We helped him apply to colleges and ensured he had the fees needed for the applications and the tools he needed to successfully transfer.

As he had cared for his mother and grandma all this time, they had become dependent on him and feared his leaving them. They continually told him that they couldn't live without him, that he simply could not leave them – not even for college.

The guilt would have worn most adults down, but Ralph, quietly and consistently explained how this was his life and this is what he was going to do. He had a goal, a mission, and he was not going to let anything, or anyone, including his family, get in his way.

With his goal in site, off to college Ralph went. He had earned a scholarship to pay for most of his tuition and books, but he worked to pay for his living expenses as he had no one at home to assist him. He didn't let the demands of school and work deter him. He was driven to overcome his childhood.

Upon his graduation from his undergraduate work, he stopped by to see the staff and me. He was going to fulfill his goal and go to law school, and he wanted to thank us for our support. So proud of his accomplishments, we took up a collection for a down payment for a car he was looking to purchase.

Ralph wasn't a bad kid, but his story deserves to be told in *Lessons from the Bad Kids* as he could have easily become one of the bad kids. Thanks to his internal drive and resiliency and the support he received from his friends and teachers, he became a testimony to what we all can accomplish if we remain determined – if we pick ourselves up when life knocks us down for life WILL surely knock us down.

We all know people, however, who have picked themselves up, brushed themselves off, and gone on. It usually requires someone there to encourage and support them and tell them, "You can!" All students have the potential to do anything they choose to do, but no one can succeed in isolation, no matter how resilient he or she may be. This lesson is not just ONE of the bad kids' lessons to be taught. It could truly be taught by most of the bad kids we have encountered. It is a lesson from which we could all greatly benefit.

I will use Lisa as the main instructor into this valuable lesson.

Lisa was born to a woman who had a severe drug problem, and it was clear from her first year that her mother did not want her – she much too strongly craved and needed her drugs to be bothered by having to care for and rear a child. For Lisa, there were no educational toys, stuffed animals, or stories at bedtime. Since there was no father identified, when Lisa reached school age, she was taken from her mother and sent to live with her grandmother.

Grandmother was a good woman, who worked at the local bar and just scraped by financially. She could barely provide for herself, let alone a child, so Lisa often went without. Although she cared for Lisa as best she could, she was a pragmatist, who worked most nights and did not see the value of education. She did not push Lisa to attend or succeed in school. She would often sleep late in the day since her shift ended at 3:00 a.m., and, therefore, she would often not bring Lisa to school.

Yet, Lisa liked going when she could and would do her best while she was there even though it was apparent she would not do well academically due to her lack of attendance and lack of homework assistance. Lisa seemed to recognize the importance of education and wanted the normalcy that went along with education – she wanted the life the other children seemed to have.

As a result of Lisa's positive attitude, she managed to progress through grade school and entered the middle school hopeful of her possibilities.

Lisa's first year of middle school, her grandmother married, and while she worked, her new husband was to watch Lisa and help her with her homework. Unfortunately, the man grandmother married was not a good man, and he began to sexually abuse Lisa. One day at school, Lisa started to cry and her teacher sent her to the counselor to whom Lisa reported the abuse.

The authorities were called, and Lisa was taken out of the home and sent to another town where she didn't know anyone while they investigated.

Grandfather was arrested, and Grandmother felt horrible. She felt extremely guilty that she had brought such a man into the house.

To add to Lisa's trauma, a long, drawn out, ugly hearing was held where she was required to testify to all he had done to her. She had to relive the horrific details over and over again before he was found guilty and sentenced to jail.

After he was sent to jail, Lisa was returned to her grandmother's where she felt guilty like many victims do, thinking it was her fault that her grandmother had lost her husband in spite of her grandmother's insistence that wasn't the case. They danced the dance of both feeling guilty to the point where they simply could not talk to each other, and the home became a very quiet home indeed.

At school, Lisa fell behind. She tried so hard and had a positive attitude when her depression or anxiety allowed her. She wanted so badly to graduate and go on to school to become a nurse as she continued to long for the normalcy of the other students' lives, but she just couldn't keep up with the work due to her absences and depression.

During the end of her sophomore year, Lisa showed up in the counseling office to request a transfer to our school. She was determined to find a way to graduate and move forward with her life in spite of the curve balls she had been thrown in life.

At Lisa's intake, I knew immediately she was going to succeed at our school. She had an inner strength, a determination. Her enthusiasm and positive energy filled the room as she explained that she was going to graduate early, so she could start at the college a year early. She explained she wanted to be out on her own; she didn't want to be a burden on her grandmother or anyone. She wanted a normal life, and if life wouldn't give it to her, she would go out and grab it for herself.

True to her word, in spite of ups and downs with depression, with the help of her teachers, outside sexual assault counselors, and me, Lisa graduated a year early and actually gave the graduation speech that year.

As I listened to her speak, I was reminded of Lisa's lesson for all of us; she knew perseverance and resiliency would bring her life's riches. In spite of having to deal with her mother's drug addiction, abandonment, poverty, abuse, the court system, and depression, Lisa was a survivor. She always exhibited resiliency and found her inner strength and dreams to push her forward. I always told her she was the whole package – beautiful, smart, likable, strong, and resilient.

The bad kids are a special breed. I see it all the time. The names and the stories may change, but the common denominator I see all the time is rich resiliency. They are survivors – no matter what life throws their way, they will face it head on and will land on their feet. These so-called bad kids are truly quite the role models for us all.

Resiliency isn't always intrinsic for all students. Sometimes we have to help create it by providing the tools and the skills necessary to survive life's daily challenges. I am not sure why, but for some reason, there has been a huge increase in the number of students attending our school who suffer from extreme anxiety.

My heart breaks for these students as they are so insecure and unsure of themselves, they lack the confidence that they can do anything, and they suffer such depression or anxiety that they literally become paralyzed.

When I first encountered Carolyn at her intake, I had a hard time getting her to look at me or talk to me. She was so timid that she did her best to blend into the chair and disappear. Her mom fervently requested independent studies in order to address her daughter's anxiety, and I did my best to fight it. I explained that the worst thing that could happen would be for us to allow Carolyn to run away and disappear. I assured her I was confident we could assimilate her into our family and help her with both her anxiety and depression symptoms. After much discussion, I finally convinced both Carolyn and her mother to give us a one-week trial.

I met her at the bus her first day and welcomed her to our campus. I gave her a tour of the school and introduced her to all her teachers whom I had frontloaded about Carolyn and her condition. I showed her where the bathrooms were and where breakfast and lunch were served. I explained the process for going to individual tutoring, to lie down, to see me, to use the restroom, and to get help when she was feeling overwhelmed or anxious. I explained at our school it was okay to just walk out of a classroom and come to my office at any time if needed. I sat down and helped her begin to plan her academic plan, introduced her to a few students who I knew would befriend her, and I told her I would check in on her each period to see how she was doing.

When I left her with Mrs. Taylor for the remainder of the period, I could see the fear in her eyes, but I knew she was in good hands. I knew we had this.

I checked in with Carolyn each period to see how she was doing, and she indicated she was okay each period. I looked for her at lunch, and lo and behold, she was sitting with a couple of students who had seen her sitting alone and had gone over to welcome her. I stopped and gave a moment of thanks for our students and their kindness and slowly walked away without saying anything, leaving them to their questioning, sharing, and giggling.

That night Carolyn's mom called me. When I heard her voice, I got a pit in my stomach, worried there was a problem. To my delight, however, she had called to thank me. She said Carolyn had had a great day and had actually been texting with some of the students that night.

She said it was the first time her daughter hadn't come home full of anxiety and in tears. She said Carolyn was actually excited to return the next day and had even done a little homework.

It would be nice if I could simply end the story here and applaud our success at acclimating Carolyn and say that her anxiety and depression dissipated and all went well from this moment forward. Unfortunately, that is not how anxiety and depression work. They don't just go away because one has a supportive, nurturing environment and caring people in one's life. No, depression and anxiety are much stronger than that, and one day, Carolyn showed up in my office, hyperventilating and crying. That was the day, Carolyn taught me her lesson.

When I saw her, standing in my office door, shaking with tears rolling down her face, I wasn't initially sure what to do, so I just went to her and hugged her and told her that at that moment all we had to worry about was breathing. I told her nothing else mattered in that moment. We just had to breathe.

So as I held her, I took in a deep breath and slowly released it, counting to ten with each breath. Slowly she started to emulate me, and eventually, we were breathing in unison. As this happened, I noticed the pit in my stomach disappeared. It was not only making Carolyn feel better, it was putting me at ease.

Once she was able to breathe regularly, I could tell she still wasn't willing or able to talk, so I told her I needed to do a few things before I could sit down and talk with her, and I asked her to color until I was available.

And with that, we created a system that worked for Carolyn and eventually for most of our students who suffered from anxiety; and a system that taught me a valuable life lesson: When life gets overwhelming, we must remember to breathe, first and foremost, and then we must remember to take a moment to remember the beauty in life. Carolyn taught me that if we do these two things, we truly can face anything.

Carolyn was an amazing young woman who taught me another lesson later in her tenure.

After one of her anxiety attacks, she and I were talking, and I was listing all her amazing attributes. She was intelligent, she was extremely talented artistically, she was organized and efficient, she was kind and caring, she was beautiful.

As I listed, she looked at me as if I were speaking another language. When I stopped and asked her what was the matter, she looked down, and tears started to flow down her checks. After sometime, she said, "I just don't think any of that is true. I just don't know that person you are describing."

I thought about that for a minute and responded, "Whenever you doubt yourself, whenever you can't see your beauty, please, please, take a moment and pretend you are me and then look at yourself through my eyes because my eyes see ... my eyes see your strength, your talent, and your beauty. My eyes see the truth."

This exercise of pausing and actually imagining switching roles and viewing herself from my eyes worked for Carolyn. It was a tangible exercise that helped her get through the dark times, and it was a moment that taught me another lesson: We all have moments of doubt and weakness, and when we do, we need to pause a moment and see ourselves through our loved one's eyes. If we do, we will see our strength, our talent, and our true beauty, and we will be able to go on and face all life throws our way.

Rob Beckwith

Rob Beckwith

Chapter 10

Reinforcements

Another lesson the bad kids have taught us is we can't make it in life alone. We need others. Human beings are very social creatures. Whether we like it or not, we are interdependent. Sometimes we have to seek help beyond our own circles; sometimes we need to call in reinforcements. Coaches know this, doctors certainly know this, military leaders live this, and it is vital that we as educators and individuals embrace this.

As we have shown throughout this book, each individual can make a huge difference in other's lives by simply being there, listening, and offering guidance and positive reinforcements, but no one can do or be it all in every instance. No one has all the answers or is able to handle all the problems by oneself.

Our staff meets weekly to discuss all the students and brainstorm the best strategies for each child. When most of the staff is ready to throw in the towel on a student, one of us always says, "Well, what if we try [this or that]?" And it breathes fresh air into the room, and we all commit to trying again. We couldn't do that as individuals. We need each other. We need to be a team and bounce ideas off each other, and we need to feel safe to ask for help. But even within our staff, we can't always handle all the issues that come our way.

Sometimes we have to recognize that a student needs more than we can offer. Of course anytime we suspect any form of child abuse or neglect, it is our obligation under the law to contact the Child Protective Services. We need to ensure our pride doesn't ever get in the way, and we need to error on the side of caution, reporting any time we have any suspicion of abuse or neglect. We might not always get the response we desire, but it is our duty to report.

We also need to reach outside our own circle and seek outside reinforcements when we are handling mental health issues for which we cannot ensure the safety of the child.

When Trisha shared with me she hated herself and her life and had been cutting to gain control, she eventually showed me that she had carved, "BIG FAT UGLY BITCH" on her stomach. I knew immediately I was out of my league, and I needed help.

When Ester showed me the bruises on her neck, thighs, and arms that her boyfriend had caused, I knew I had to seek expert support.

When Tom told me he didn't want to live anymore and shared his suicide fantasy in detail, I knew he needed more help than I could give.

When Jarrod cried in my office that he desperately wanted to stop using meth, but he just couldn't find the way, I knew I could help him, but I couldn't do it alone. I needed the help of outside resources.

This is equally true not just for high school students but also when dealing with parents, grandparents, and guardians of younger elementary students. At the elementary level, it is frequently the custodial adults who reach out to educators for help. They are lost in a world they have never traveled. They know where to send their children to get an education, but they don't know what reinforcements are available or how to access them, so they reach out to us.

When the grandmother of seven came in to school to bring a loaf of bread and peanut butter, so her recently obtained grandchildren could eat, it was apparent she was struggling to do it all on her own, and I knew she needed help. Having no previous knowledge of the system and the supports available, she obviously worried how she was going to meet all the kids' needs. We filled out the free lunch form together, and I put her in touch with Social Services and the state Medi-Cal contact. She wanted to meet the kids' needs, and she could, but she needed reinforcements.

When Ricky's mental health issues escalated and impacted the rest of the family so much so that his mom came in battered and bruised, crying that she could no longer control her baby boy, it was time to place a call and get help for both the family and for Ricky.

When the tragic, accidental death of one of our students impacted the lives and education of our students and teachers, I knew I couldn't comfort, reassure, and help everyone alone. The crisis team needed to be called to ensure our family, including me, could grieve, begin to heal, and move forward.

By the same token, as much as we need to seek help and bring in reinforcements when our students, our guardians, and we need it, we must also understand that we need to be those reinforcements for others in our communities. We can do this in various ways.

At Black Rock, the community blood bank knows that they can reach out and get reinforcements from the students' blood donations. Our elementary schools have been used as evacuation areas in times of natural disasters, both in earthquakes and in fires. Our students complete seventy-five hours of community service as a graduation requirement, so individuals, organizations, and businesses know they can contact the school and get the reinforcements they need.

It is important to create a cycle of giving and taking, teaching the students that they must give back to the community if they expect the community to be there for them in their times of need.

The bad kids are sometimes wise beyond their years. They know they can't make it alone. They know they must reach out to others and get reinforcements if they hope to survive. This is a valuable lesson for both educators and individuals.

If we could all keep our egos out of the equation when seeking solutions to life's problems, it would be easier to ask for help when we needed it. We could save ourselves a great deal of unnecessary hardship and heartache if we sought outside help and support. We are simply not meant to tackle life and all its ups and downs alone.

Lowkey Pictures

Rob Beckwith

Conclusion

And now we get to the, "So what?" You may have read this book for a variety of reasons: You may have seen the movie *The Bad Kids* and were inspired to know more about these cast off students. You may be a teacher who experiences these students in your classroom, and you are determined to help them succeed. You may be a school administrator who wants to prevent your students from being sent to the office, suspended and expelled, or lost as drop outs. You may be a student yourself who wants to be part of the solution, who wants to help make the world a little better. You may be a mental health worker who knows you too can make a difference in these kids' lives, or you may be a mom or dad who simply desires to learn from others to make your loved one's lives and your life better.

Regardless of the reason why you originally embarked on this journey into the lives of the bad kids, we have now reached the point for your decision. These are just a few of the kids' stories. There are many, many more out there. Are these kids who have gotten in trouble in school and in the community and fallen behind in their studies bad kids? Do they wake up each morning determined to let us down and hurt us, or is it society who has let them down and hurt them?

To paraphrase the author and behavioral scientist, Steve Maraboli, if we refuse to look at these kids in a new light and we only see them for what they were, only see them for the mistakes they made, we will be making a very grave mistake indeed.

It is time for us, as a society, to change our perspective. These children, our students, are the future we are helping to create.

The Japanese fill cracks in their pottery with gold as "they believe when something has suffered damage and has a history, it becomes more beautiful" (Barbara Bloom).

If we fill these children's cracks with gold, we can create great pieces of art and a beautiful future.

The Bad Kids is a call to action for all of us. In all honesty, in our combined sixty-plus years in education, we have rarely, if ever, met a bad kid. Mostly, we have met a lot of children and young adults who have been put into very, very difficult situations. Their responses to these situations may not always be the best. Their decisions may not always be the best, but these reactions do not make them bad kids. Mostly, they are just kids who are calling out, crying out, for our help. It is up to us.

If we take the time to listen and then listen more closely, these bad kids will not only tell us what we need to know to help them, they will give us lessons to improve ourselves as individuals and our world as a whole. If we don't listen, it will not be a story of bad kids but rather a story of the *bad society* or *bad future*.

If we don't act to help both these individuals and this population as a whole, we will simply perpetuate the problems for both them as individuals and for our society as a whole.

Emerson once said, "The secret of success in society is a certain heartiness and sympathy" (Emerson, 1844). Far be it from us to correct Emerson; true, in order to succeed, we do indeed need to have heart, but rather than sympathy, we truly need a certain amount of empathy and compassion.

We can start on a small scale in our daily lives, making a difference in our loved one's lives and in the lives of people with whom we work and come in contact. We can pause and try to put ourselves in their shoes before we act. That in itself can and will make a big difference.

We can also start to work with our communities, our local school systems, and our local, state, and federal policy makers to spotlight this issue rather than labeling these kids and throwing them out with the trash.

It is our strong desire as educators that you now be able to answer THE question whole-heartedly, knowing indeed there is no such thing as a bad kid.

Lowkey Pictures

About the Authors

Vonda Viland has led the Morongo Unified School District's alternative program for at-risk students for the past five years, working with students who have been disenfranchised from the traditional school system. Approximately 90 percent of her student body lives below the poverty level with many struggling to deal with issues no child should have to face, including abuse, neglect, parenthood, depression, anxiety, and addiction.

She and her staff have developed an individualized program where they work to educate the child, not just teach the curriculum. Living in such a remote area with extremely limited resources, she and her staff work hard to meet the educational, emotional, and physical needs of their students.

Vonda and her staff and students were the subjects of the new Sundance award-winning documentary film *The Bad Kids*, which features her educational approach and offers viewers a practical model for how public education can address and combat the crippling effects of poverty in the lives of American schoolchildren.

As a secondary English teacher for sixteen years, Vonda received the Commitment to Excellence Award from the California Middle School Foundation and Partnership and was recognized as teacher of the year for the California League of Middle Schools Region 10. After earning her Master's Degree in School Administration from California State University, she has worked as a site administrator at the elementary, secondary, and continuation levels.

Deborah Turner is a lifetime educator and learner. Graduating from Bowling Green University in Ohio with a B.S. in Education, she made the move to California and found work as an elementary teacher in a socioeconomically depressed, rural, remote area of the desert. Dr. Turner quickly grasped the need to be more than a teacher to these at-risk students.

Seeking to improve her skills, she obtained her Masters in Educational Administration from California State University, San Bernardino. Becoming the principal of a small elementary school right out of the classroom, she and her team of teachers brought the school out of Program Improvement and set the students on the road to success.

Obtaining her doctorate in Organizational Leadership from La Verne University, she co-authored the book, *Building a Bridge to Success, from Program Improvement to Excellence*, based on her research and experience. Recognizing the need to address student needs at a deeper level, she became the director and subsequently the assistant superintendent of Instructional Services in the largest area district in the state of California. Working with staff and students has been her passion for over thirty-four years, and she is proud of all the bad kids who have gone on to reach for success.